Practical
Ethnography

Practical
Ethnography
A Guide to Doing Ethnography in the Private Sector

Sam Ladner

Routledge
Taylor & Francis Group

LONDON AND NEW YORK

First published 2014 by Left Coast Press, Inc.

Published 2016 by Routledge
2 Park Square, Milton Park, Abingdon, Oxon OX14 4RN
711 Third Avenue, New York, NY 10017, USA

Routledge is an imprint of the Taylor & Francis Group, an informa business

Library of Congress Cataloging-in-Publication Data
Ladner, Sam.
    Practical ethnography : a guide to doing ethnography in the private sector / Sam Ladner.
        pages cm.
    Summary: "Ethnography is an increasingly important research method in the private
sector, yet ethnographic literature continues to focus on an academic audience. Sam Ladner
fills the gap by advancing rigorous ethnographic practice that is tailored to corporate settings
where colleagues are not steeped in social theory, research time lines may be days rather than
months or years, and research sponsors expect actionable outcomes and recommendations.
Ladner provides step-by-step guidance at every turn—covering core methods, research
design, using the latest mobile and digital technologies, project and client management,
ethics, reporting, and translating your findings into business strategies. This book is the
perfect resource for private-sector researchers, designers, and managers seeking robust
ethnographic tools or academic researchers hoping to conduct research in corporate settings.
More information on the book is available at http://www.practicalethnography.com/"
—Provided by publisher.
    Includes bibliographical references and index.
    ISBN 978-1-61132-389-4 (hardback)—ISBN 978-1-61132-390-0 (paperback)—ISBN 978-1-
61132-391-7 (eBook institutional)—ISBN 978-1-61132-741-0 (eBook consumer)
    1. Business anthropology—Research—Methodology. 2. Ethnology—Research—
Methodology. I. Title.
    GN450.8.L33 2014
    305.80072′1—dc23
                                        2013044337

ISBN Hardback (978-1-61132-389-4)
ISBN Paperback (978-1-61132-390-0)

Cover and text design by Hannah Jennings

To every single one of the people I have met in my research.
Your stories make me know what it means to be a human.

Contents

Chapter 1
Introduction

I remember the exact moment when I discovered the power of observing. I was in journalism school. Our professor, Eugene, was a veteran newspaperman, the kind of guy who'd give you props for a well-placed comma. He taught "print reporting," as it was called back then, but what he was really teaching us was how to notice things.

Eugene used an old-fashioned lectern. He'd stand there at the front of the room, looking at us sternly through his glasses, his hands resting at the top of the lectern. He had a habit of rolling up his shirtsleeves when he was about to make an important point. That day, we were reviewing a selection of newspaper stories he'd selected for us to read. When he started to roll up his sleeves, I started paying attention.

Eugene was reviewing a story about a police officer who was killed in his car. The journalist described how the officer was found, sitting in his car with, "his finger still hooked into the handle of his coffee cup." Eugene looked up from his lectern. "What did you notice about this story?" he asked.

The finger still hooked into the coffee cup was a colorful detail. Indeed, that's exactly what Eugene told us: details offer color. He pointed out that we could see a picture in our minds with details like that. He said it didn't hurt that it was a cop drinking coffee—it plays off the stereotype.

Practical Ethnography: A Guide to Doing Ethnography in the Private Sector by Sam Ladner, 11–20. © 2014 Left Coast Press, Inc. All rights reserved.

I used that trick myself in a story adding the "detail" of a toothpick. I wrote a story about a middle-aged man learning to read. I wrote that he "took the toothpick out of his mouth and then explained" something. I even got noticed by a big-shot editor for that detail. I didn't know it at the time, but it was my first lesson in the power of observation.

My first lesson—and I learned it wrong.

There's more to ethnography than merely seeing "details." Details are description. Ethnography goes further; it provides explanation. Ethnography is about understanding meaning, not just "details." Ethnographers connect details to wider patterns of social life. Mere details can be gathered into lists and reported back. The cop's finger was hooked into his coffee cup. So what? What does this mean? It could mean he wasn't expecting violence. It could mean he was caught by surprise. The detail of the coffee cup has *meaning*. It is the ethnographer's job to explain that meaning.

This is exactly what anthropologist Clifford Geertz (2000) meant when he described culture as "webs of significance that man himself [*sic*] has spun." What Geertz is saying is that culture is about the meaning we collectively ascribe to objects, people, and events. Culture is about meaning, and ethnography is a method to explain that meaning. Details are not meaning; they are just a list of things that happened.

The difference between "noticing things" and ethnography is that ethnographers make every attempt to decipher the meaning of a vague European accent or a nervous, bouncy knee. One must explain the significance of the bouncy knee: before a race, in a doctor's office, or at a family dinner. The ethnographer puts her opinions on the line; she suggests a meaning. She is not content to "let the reader decide" what this thing means. She will make an effort to explain, not simply describe.

This is a terribly difficult endeavor, in so many ways. How do you know what's important and what isn't? I've seen many novice researchers become overwhelmed quickly in the field. They begin to "notice" everything, relevant or not. They are quickly weighed down by meaningless and endless field notes. They miss things sitting right in front of them because they're too busy trying to notice things.

In some ways, explanation is doubly hard in private-sector ethnography. Academic ethnographers use social theory and rigorous method to avoid the "noticing everything" problem, but they also have the luxury of longer timelines. Private-sector ethnographers must adapt academic theory, method, and timelines to suit their research needs. Designers have taken up ethnography keenly in the private sector, and understandably so; they are natural observers. Designers tend to notice "details" like buttons that don't work, signs that point the wrong direction, and error messages that make no sense. Noticing how things are broken is an important trait in a designer, but it is not enough for ethnography. Ethnographers must explain why that error message makes no sense, in that particular context for those particular people. Good explanations provide general principles that can then be applied to other design problems. Poor explanations only work for that one instance or context.

This book is a practical guide to doing ethnography in the private sector. It is written for two kinds of people. First, I am writing for social scientists who want to take their skills out of academia and into the corporate setting. This is a largely pragmatic reaction to the virtual disintegration of the academic job market. In 1975, 57% percent of faculty were either tenured or on the tenure track. By 2009, that number had fallen to 31% percent (Wilson, 2010). That leaves two-thirds of PhDs with few options other than the private sector, yet few of their professors have any private-sector experience or familiarity.

You may be an anthropologist or sociologist and you want to adapt your research skills to the applied setting. You are probably familiar with social theory and method, but have never provided specific product or design recommendations. Your supervisors have little to no advice to give you about embarking on this journey. This book will help you translate your knowledge and skills into a practical application. It might also teach you how to create a job or a business that uses your academic skills. Your skills will help you become a research consultant, market researcher, or even a product designer. You will get the most value out of the chapters on tools, managing clients, and this chapter, which describes why ethnography is gaining popularity in the private sector, and how to increase its uptake even further.

Second, I am also writing for people who are already working in the private sector but may not have robust academic training in the ethnographic method. You could be a product manager, a designer, or a market researcher. You want to deploy the innovative power of ethnography, but you need a practical, step-by-step guide to help you do it. This book will help you improve your research skills. It will also help you get organizational buy-in for using ethnography as a method for innovation, design, or consumer insight. You will get the most value out of this introductory chapter and the theory chapter, which explain what ethnography is and why it differs from other research methods. You will also benefit from the step-by-step chapters on how to do ethnography and produce deliverables.

Feel free to skip around this book. Take your time, skip the parts that lack relevance for you. This book is not a scholarly textbook. It is not intended as a guide to academic research, nor is it an academic meditation on methodology itself. My goal with this book is to improve the quality and rigor of ethnographic research in the corporate setting—not to debate the arcane intricacies of academic debates. Academics wanting that kind of literature review are encouraged to look elsewhere.

What Comes Next

This book is organized loosely around the steps of a typical corporate ethnography project. I start with the intellectual heritage of ethnography and explain why ethnography is relatively uncommon in the corporate sector. I then offer readers an argument in favor of using theory in this kind of research, and a selection of social theory that I have used for my own corporate ethnography practice. Specifically, I cover concepts such as social capital, gender, economic class, and the presentation of self as tools for organizing and cohering your ethnographic research before you go into the field. From there, I follow the steps of a typical ethnographic project, from project management to technology and tools to client management and reporting. I show readers the nuts and bolts of a well-run ethnographic project. Unlike academic textbooks, I show ethnographers how to work in the culture of the private sector, the pitfalls to avoid, and the different kinds of reports and deliverables you can produce. In the final chapters of this book, I extend the ethnographic lens to other methods, including online research, focus groups, and usability studies.

What Is Ethnography?

Ethnography is the study of culture. It is from the Greek "ethno," meaning folk or culture, and "grapho," meaning writing. Historically, it has meant simply "writing about culture," although today there are other ways to tell ethnographic stories, including audio, video, and even graphic novels. Ethnography's history as a method is one of long term, academic commitment. It is no wonder it is difficult to apply in the private sector because it was designed for the university.

Ethnography is often associated with anthropologist Branislaw Malinowski. Malinowski was born in Cracow, Poland, on April 7, 1884. He was steeped in innovative research in both his family and his university training. His father pioneered new ethnographic methods to trace the development of Slavic languages. Malinowski himself later studied mathematics and physics at Cracow's Uniwersytet Jagiellonski, the same university where the groundbreaking astronomer Nikolai Copernicus argued the earth revolved around the sun. Malinowski's scientific training taught him how to collect quantitative data and instilled in him an appreciation for the functioning of rules and regulations. But instead of becoming rules-bound in his research, Malinowski saw that rules were both followed and flouted. As his biographer Michael Young points out, Malinowski learned that "people evaded rules, almost as often as they obeyed them" (Young, 2004, p. 75). Searching for patterns, regularity, and the exceptions to that regularity became the hallmark of Malinowski's method. Eventually, Malinowski relocated to the London School of Economics, and to fieldwork in the Pacific in the Trobriand Islands. He produced the book *Argonauts of the Western Pacific*, which is often hailed as the first ethnography.[1] This book detailed the complex gift-giving activities of these islanders. Through detailed description and then explanation, Malinowski showed how culture is brought to life through everyday behaviors.

Malinowski's work inspired many anthropologists to apply the same methodical approach to understanding "exotic" cultures. Margaret Mead famously travelled to Samoa to research coming-of-age rituals. Later, she went to Bali, where she and her husband and colleague, Gregory Bateson, researched coming of age experiences. In her Bali fieldwork, Mead took 25,000 photographs, which by today's standards sounds reasonable. But in the 1920s, this meant 22,000 feet of film (over 60 football fields!) that had to be developed, printed, and annotated (Library of Congress, 2001). Imagine the prolonged effort and focus that took.

The ethnographic method is steeped in this patient approach to documenting social life and making interpretations about its meaning. Malinowski detailed the enormity of the work in a letter he wrote immediately following his fieldwork in the Trobriand Islands:

> I estimate that my future publication will be voluminous, roughly three volumes of 500 pages each at 500 words per page. It will take me about two years to get the [manuscript] ready and see it through the press. My material is now a chaotic mass of notes. To work it out and put it into the right theoretical frame is perhaps the most difficult, exacting, and important stage of research. (quoted in Young, 2004, p. 82)

Malinowski had an enormous number of "details," but the struggle was to put it "into the right theoretical frame," or to explain the meaning of these details. He persevered through a "chaotic mess of notes." It was a long commitment.

Malinowski's and Mead's brand of long-term, methodical ethnography continues in academia today. Some wonderful contemporary examples of ethnography include Paul Willis's fieldwork in British classrooms, that led to his ethnography, *Learning to Labour,* and Doug Foley's *Learning Capitalist Culture,* a 14-year odyssey with Latino youth in Texas. A team of researchers spent almost five years collecting data for their ethnography, *Crestwood Heights,* the ethnography of a Toronto-area neighborhood in the '50s. More recently, the authors of *Busier Than Ever* spent over a year in the field with the rushed families of Silicon Valley. Ethnography has even caused a sensation, as did Sudhir Venkatesh in his book, *Gang Leader for a Day,* the controversial ethnography of his experiences with Chicago drug gangs. All of these examples show the classic anthropological approach: long-term, embedded observation within the community, interviewing, the methodical collection of data, and most importantly, the constant attempt to explain what life means to these people. It is this final characteristic of ethnography—the participants' viewpoint—that is the most important reason to use ethnography in the private sector.

Ethnography's Value to the Private Sector

Academics may be surprised to learn that ethnography is now garnering attention in the business world. Rotman School of Management dean Roger Martin calls it "an essential tool" for innovation, while *Businessweek* calls it the "new core competence." Whether you are an independent ethnographer, work for a research vendor, or are an ethnographer internal to the organization, you will have "clients" in the sense that you have people who will be using your findings to design, implement, improve, or launch something. Ethnographers can help their clients in unique and powerful ways.

There are two major reasons why ethnography has recently gained popularity in the corporate world. First, ethnography is conducted in context, providing new insights into the other objects, people, and products that consumers are currently using. This *in situ* method contrasts with focus groups, surveys, and "Big Data," which take place either in a facility, or simply on the researcher's computer desktop. Ethnography, by contrast, collects direct insight about the contents and people in the consumer's home, car, or office, all of which affects consumer choice and product use. This provides opportunities for product innovation. An ethnographer may discover, for example, that parents use jerry-rigged bungee cords to strap iPads to the backs of their car seats. Children are entertained with movies, while parents can concentrate on the road. The ethnographer may conclude that there is a product opportunity: to replace these bungee cords with a customized iPad holder. This kind of insight only comes from contextual observation.

The second reason why ethnography is valuable in business is because it takes a particular stance its practitioners call the "emic" position. That is, ethnographers strive to take the participants' point of view. Sociologist Dorothy Smith calls this a "standpoint." If you take the participants' standpoint, it's possible to see what would otherwise be invisible. Ethnographers try to understand the participants' language, concepts, categories, and opinions, and use them to define their research. Focus groups, surveys, and analytics, by contrast, use the "etic" position, which is defined by the researchers. If you've ever taken a survey, only to find you don't fit neatly into one of their little boxes, you have experienced the etic position in action. The *researcher's* language, concepts, categories, and opinions shape the research. The emic position allows companies to create contextually nuanced and personalized products and services. This offers the potential of a differentiation of what Pine and Gilmore (1998) called the "experience economy" as far back as 1998. Consumers can now pick and choose between mere commodities; customized experiences require deeper insight into consumers' wants, needs, and cultures.

The emic position puts the *research participant* in the center. When ethnography is used in the private sector, this means it is the *consumer* who defines what a product means *to him or her*, which can then be interpreted and built upon by product managers and designers. Ethnography puts consumer needs first, which means a product based on ethnographic research will solve real consumer problems. Other innovation methods are usually etic; they take the company's standpoint. Innovation strategies like Six Sigma, Kaizan, and lean production start with the *company's* needs. These methods tend to have the *company's* standpoint, not the consumer's. Ethnography starts with the consumer's standpoint and defines products, services, and marketing messages according to that standpoint. Its power, then, stems fundamentally from its emic position. To illustrate the difference between emic and etic standpoints, let's use an example.

Etic Versus Emic: The Example of Starbucks

For 24 years, there was a curious phenomenon at the intersection of Robson and Thurlow streets in Vancouver. Two Starbucks sat kitty-corner to each other, one on the northeast corner, the other on the southwest. Imagine a researcher tasked with finding out which of these Starbucks is more valuable to the company. The etic researcher might start by using concepts important to the company. She may use "variables" like how many people go in and out, how many lattes versus americanos are served, how many staff work there, how much money is earned. If all these data were collected through the point of sale system, she could do her analysis without ever seeing this iconic Starbucks Corner. She may decide the southwest store is less profitable and should therefore be closed. In this view, the two stores are compared using exactly the same criteria. She may come up with an answer without ever having seen the two stores.

The etic researcher may decide which store is more valuable without even knowing the customers' standpoint.

The ethnographer, by contrast, would start by understanding what these two stores *mean to the customers*. She may collect data about the same kinds of things the etic researcher would, but her standpoint would be from the customer's perspective. She'd ask customers why they chose one store over the other. She'd observe the Harley Davidson motorcycles parked next to the store on the southwest corner. She may ask some of the bikers why they chose this store, and probe around the times they come. In the northeast store, she may notice there are more briefcases being carried into the store. She might ask people why they come to that store, only to be rebuffed with "I don't have time to talk." Her emic standpoint would tell her that people in northeast store are fast-paced, business people who see the store as a "to go" location. Her emic position may also tell her that the southwest store patrons see "their" store as a community hangout. She may conclude that the southwest store is a "community" store, while the northeast store is a "volume" store. Both stores are valuable to their customers, she would conclude, but for different reasons. Her ethnography would explain the customer perspective, and her recommendations would compare this to the company's perspective. What is important to customers? What is important to the company? How can we align these interests?

It turns out that the southwest store did indeed close in the spring of 2012. It was the end of an era. On its last day, the store's doors were ceremoniously locked for the last time. Staff members hugged longtime customers. A few tears were shed. The northeast store continues to be open.

It's unclear if an ethnographer had any role in that decision, but if she had, it would have been difficult to deny that the bikers now have nowhere to park their Harleys while they pick up a latte. Did Starbucks make a mistake with this decision? Starbucks CEO Howard Shultz noted that overexpansion was one of the major threats to the Starbucks brand. He argues in his 2011 book that the company does not sell coffee so much as the experience of coffee (Schultz, 2011). Without knowing much about how this particular decision was made, I would argue this was likely a hard decision, but perhaps one that missed the opportunity to cement the brand as one devoted to experiences instead of products.

The emic perspective often throws a wrench into the typical corporate decision-making process. What is "true" to a customer may not be "true" to the company. In the next chapter, I'll explain that there are indeed several ways to think about "truth." "Ethnographic truth" is a distinct kind of truth that differs from traditional market research. And it needs to be communicated differently.

Chapter 2
Using Theory in Ethnography

How do researchers know if their findings are "true"? I never considered that question—until I took a research methods class in graduate school. I learned that there is more than one way to judge research validity. My professor, Catherine, was the first person to show me that different kinds of research produce different kinds of "truth."

Catherine had the unfortunate habit of terrifying me with her intelligence. One day, Catherine wore her navy blue suit and looked every bit the part of the elder stateswoman. She was explaining what it meant to know something is true—at least that's what I thought she was explaining. It all got a bit fuzzy when she used the word "verisimilitude." I almost passed out from the fear. This was the beginning of my intellectual journey to ethnography.

We must all grapple with terrifyingly complex ideas in order to become good ethnographers. Becoming a good private-sector ethnographer means you must understand your research method *and* be able to explain it to your clients and stakeholders. Practically speaking, this means you must know how to do ethnography but also how to *think about* ethnography. It demands of us a higher order level of understanding. We have already discussed the "emic" orientation of ethnography. This standpoint necessarily shapes the way we research and the theories we use to interpret our findings. In this chapter, I introduce you to a kind of truth not common to the private sector, but one to which most ethnographers subscribe. I then offer a set of theories that will help you find this kind of truth in your research projects. By the end of this chapter, you should be able to select a theoretical framework for a practical ethnography project, and explain why you chose that framework instead of a theory more suited to quantitative method. You will not only understand ethnography, but be able to explain it to others.

Finding Meaning Versus Finding Facts

"Truth" in most private-sector organizations involves the compilation of "facts" about observable events. This is usually called the "positivist" perspective, and it usually (though not always) involves numbers. I like the way Finnish cultural theorist Alasuutari (1995) describes positivism as the "factist" view. The factist view assumes there is a "truth" about a given topic, and the researcher's role is to discover this truth. It is the same orientation that a natural scientist would have toward her subject of study—say, fungi. There are fungi. We can discover how long they take to grow. That is a fact. There are people we call consumers. We can discover how many times they purchased our product. That is also a fact.

The factist view's limitation is that it considers the study of fungi and people to be exactly the same. I was always uncomfortable with this view, having witnessed firsthand the complexity of human behavior. Certainly, when a consumer purchases a product, we can all agree that is a fact. But what thoughts and opinions came before that purchase? What does this product actually mean to that person? Is that meaning a fact? Calling that meaning a fact seems strange. We have many phenomena that are unintelligible through the factist lens. The significance of a piece of art is not a fact, for example. Opinions, preferences, affinities are not facts, but expressions of human experience. If you buy a product, that is a fact. But in the *process* of buying a product, a consumer makes sense of the product and derives meaning from it. This line of thinking is not about facts so much as it is about determining what is significant. Qualitative research can be thought of as "procedures for counting to one. Deciding what to count as a unit of analysis is fundamentally an interpretive issue requiring judgment and choice," according to ethnographer John Van Maanen (Van Maanen,

Manning, and Miller, 1986, p. 5). In other words, we are not accumulating or counting facts, but deciding what is significant.

The factist approach also assumes that people's actions can be predicted. Sociologists Potter and Lopez (2001) call this the "sin of actualism." They might agree that "How many people entered this store today?" can indeed be observed and counted reliably. But they would disagree that using these data, you can reliably predict how many people will go to this store tomorrow or the next day, or how many people would go into the same store built in another location. The social world is far too complex to make precise judgments such as these. Certainly, you can infer and make reasonable, educated guesses, but the factist view assumes there is a "right" answer that will lead to accurate predictions. I have always found this position very difficult to defend, in part because it is etic, but also because it is many times patently false.

It is a little terrifying to let go of pursuing facts and prediction. But facts and prediction are not the only value research can bring. Renouncing that school of thought leads to a whole new world of insight and a different kind of truth—truth about understanding, unriddling, decoding, and deciphering. If you believe that accurate predictions are not actually possible, your goals change. Instead of the "right" answer, you seek depth of understanding. This other kind of truth is about deep understanding. Sociologist Max Weber used the German word *verstehen* to describe his goal, which was to understand a single phenomenon as representative or indicative of a wider system. We need these interpretations just as much as we need predictions. In the absence of deep understanding, predictions are tragically uninformed. Most of us did not predict the 2008 financial meltdown, just as we did not predict the 1997 financial crisis. As Nassim Taleb tells us in his hugely influential book, *The Black Swan* (Taleb, 2007), prediction is only possible if you have a total understanding of all variables involved. This is difficult even if you study fungi, but it is nearly impossible if you study people. Accurate prediction is so rare that it virtually never happens. So forget prediction. Go for deep understanding.

Ethnographers start with Weber's notion of truth, which is often called the "interpretivist" view. An interpretivist is interested in understanding what the world means to people. Ethnographers believe that people create meaning about their own worlds in their everyday activities. This is the very definition of culture, as defined by anthropologist Clifford Geertz. He argues that culture is the meaning people ascribe to objects, people, activities, and institutions. Ethnographers uncover this meaning. Alasuutari says we "unriddle" that meaning. Is this meaning "true"? If it is true to the consumers, then what does it matter? As many a marketer has said, "Perception is reality." The private-sector ethnographer's task, then, is not to find the "truth" about products and services, but the *meanings* consumers ascribe to them. This is where the *explanation* of ethnography comes from.

Positivists rule in the private sector. Interpretivists are few in number and small in influence. Most marketers, business strategists, and product managers don't understand the interpretivist point of view, not because it is incorrect, but because it has an unfamiliar conception of truth. The "validity" of research in the private sector usually hinges on how predictive that research is, not how well it interprets the meaning of a particular product. Yet, there is a deep history of the interpretivist point of view in the marketing literature. Consumer culture theory, for example, is a theoretically robust set of literature that is over 20 years old and has its own scholarly journal, the *Journal of Consumer Culture* (Arnold and Thompson, 2005). The interpretivist view may be unusual, but it is intellectually defensible and theoretically sophisticated.

Marketers coming from the factist perspective might begin with the assumption that there is a truth to be discovered that has predictive power. The factist project of prediction lends itself to quantitative measurements. Factists implicitly believe that a demographic variable like household income will affect a product purchase. Variables like gender and ethnicity may also be discovered and used to predict a purchase. Price point is likely also part of a factist analysis. But this approach finds it difficult to operationalize social significance, social context, and the meaning consumers ascribe to products. Without this insight, the customer experience is rarely understood in any deep way. Factists struggle to explain why, say, a sign-up process doesn't work for consumers, and what principles should be used to fix it.

As an interpretivist, the private-sector ethnographer looks to theories that help uncover meanings *about products*. The private-sector ethnographer's essential point of departure is simple: the meanings consumers ascribe to products are not a "given." Just as sociologists Berger and Luckman (1966) argue, our job is to reveal the "taken for grantedness" of everyday life. A consumer finds meaning in a product. This meaning is not solely about its price, as a factist might argue. The price is important, to be sure, but what the product signifies goes far beyond its mere cost.

A product's meaning is a function of a consumer's perception of two broad concepts: 1) his own identity; and 2) the system of meaning in which he finds himself. In other words, consumers make products meaningful depending on how they see themselves and their cultural context. Accordingly, ethnographic research begins with questions such as, how does a consumer see himself? In which context does he use this product? How do identity and context interact to affect this sensemaking process?

Nuance and subtlety are difficult for our minds to parse. We collectively search for patterns of being in the world to help us minimize the cognitive load on our puny human brains. It is a comfort to always know how one greets a woman, for example, with a "Hello Ma'am." It is good to have a script on how to treat a "rich" customer with a dose of dignified deference. Eventually, these roles become fixed metaphors in our collective minds. They are an easy script we can turn to when in doubt of how to act socially. As Berger and Luckman put it, conceiving of social roles as static helps alleviate us from making "all those decisions" of how we interact (Berger and Luckman, 1966).

The ethnographer assumes that social life is in flux. This means that identity and context are understood as dynamic, fluid phenomena that may or may not conform to a fixed or "normal" definition. Fixed identities such as "women" or "Latinos" are not categories that determine behavior so much as they are roles that individuals must interpret, find meaning in, and grapple with. Not all Latinos speak Spanish. Not all women know how to put on make-up. Individuals must grapple with their membership in a category and the role that it entails. Likewise, private-sector ethnographers also assume that the social context is in flux. A household that is about to move house, or to start school, or to welcome an aging parent will have differing concerns. So we must unriddle how the consumer's identity shapes his interpretation of a particular product, and the social context in which this meaning is negotiated. What values, norms, beliefs, and behaviors are expected in this context? And how do those expectations relate to the consumer's own identity?

A Dynamic Theory of Identity

Erving Goffman offers us a theory of identity that aligns with the ethnographer's assumptions. Goffman also assumes that social life is in flux and that identity is fluid. His gift to social theory ultimately boils down to one fantastic metaphor: social life as theatre. In his book, *The Presentation of Self in Everyday Life* (Goffman, 1959), Goffman outlined this "dramaturgical" theory of social life. He argued we perform different roles on different "fronts." A front is a location that calls for a particular mode of being or presentation of self. This front has "costumes" appropriate to that location. It has a script, stage directions, and décor. A "self" is a function of which front one finds oneself in. It is not a fixed phenomenon, but one that is constructed according to context.

Take the "front" of a drycleaner's, for example. The shop owner has a "front stage" self she uses when speaking to customers. She is solicitous. She is knowledgeable and friendly. She has a "back stage" self she uses in the back room of the shop, when talking with her co-workers. Here, she may be sullen, sarcastic, or even ribald. She has an entirely different "front stage" self when she goes to the doctor's office, and speaks to the receptionist. She is demanding and impatient. She has another "back stage" self when she sits in the exam room waiting for her doctor. Here, she may be worried or anxious. These selves are all perfectly natural, even though they may conflict. A drycleaner can be a shop owner, a patient, a mother, a bank customer, and a subway rider. These are all different roles with different fronts, yet she does not feel schizophrenic or troubled by these different selves. We regularly and normally engage in "impression management" to control who sees what, when.

Goffman was particularly intrigued by instances of embarrassment or humiliation. He argued that these incidents happen when an officious front-stage self "slips" and the back-stage self is revealed. A judge's robe may fall off, revealing the plain white t-shirt of her back-stage self. A particularly hilarious example comes from an episode of *30 Rock*. The show focuses on the unlikely friendship between socially maladroit comedy writer, Liz Lemon, played by Tina Fey, and the smooth, commanding media CEO Jack Donaghey, played by Alec Baldwin. Jack is set to give a speech to his employees. He is fitted with a microphone before slipping into the men's room to freshen up. Tragically, the mic picks up the pep talk he gives to his back-stage self. His hilarious and embarrassing self-talk is transmitted to the ballroom, where all his employees can hear him. Donaghey has revealed his back-stage self, but Liz Lemon saves him by giving an even more embarrassing front-stage slip: Liz rips open her shirt on stage.

Goffman also argued that we strive to keep our fronts separate. He called this "audience segregation," or the fine art of "not crossing the streams" of our various social spheres. This collision of fronts occurs most often online. Facebook's ill-fated advertising platform, Beacon, forced a collision of fronts when it automatically broadcasted its users' purchasing behavior to all of their Facebook friends. Imagine your Goth friend's "liking" of Netflix's *The Notebook* as it was automatically posted to her newsfeed. Or your office co-worker's purchase of *Fifty Shades of Grey* automatically posted to her newsfeed. This is a collision of fronts, and it is embarrassing, even shameful. Facebook was forced to discontinue Beacon.

Applying Goffman's theory to private-sector ethnography would entail understanding impression management and the fronts in which a product is used. What is the appropriate décor of this front? What kinds of activities or objects would force a slippage and therefore embarrassment? Ethnographers should look for moments their participants describe as embarrassing or uncomfortable. This could be when they are required to provide private information in a public place, such as over the phone while inside a mobile phone store. It could also be an impression management "problem" of mixing identities, such as being forced to use an older, less "professional" username because it's convenient for the company and not the user. It could also mean a consumer being forced to share purchasing behavior widely, instead of only with a select few people. Ethnographers can discover these "slips" by asking specifically about embarrassment or by probing around customer dissatisfaction that may be due to an inadvertent humiliation.

Dynamic Theories of Identity Roles

There are several types of identity roles that are relevant to private-sector ethnography. Each of these roles can be loosely mapped back to the factist's demographic variables. But unlike the factist, the ethnographer views these identity roles as fluid. Gender, economic class, and race or ethnicity can be understood as roles that people perform, with varying degrees of success. These roles affect (but do not determine) the decision to purchase a product, how consumers use or display the product, and how they influence others to purchase the product in turn. The entire product lifecycle, from consideration to purchase to ownership to advocacy, is mediated by these roles. Individuals may subscribe to or reject outright these roles. In this way, the ethnographer sees identity roles not as independent variables that determine behavior, but as ideal types that individuals must grapple with. Products are accouterments to that grappling process. Products can assist individuals in pursuing an ideal type, or they can confound that pursuit. Private-sector ethnographers help explain these dynamic processes in terms of gender, economic class, and ethnicity roles.

Gender

First, gender roles affect how we interpret products. Those who have studied the sociology of gender know that there is a distinct difference between "sex" (which refers to a person's genitalia) and "gender" (which refers to a person's social role). Simone de Beauvoir captured this beautifully with her phrase, "One is not born a woman, but becomes one." By this she is saying that being a "woman" is something one learns to do, and is not a biologically determined phenomenon. Yet, we tend to take for granted the role of "woman" because it's less complicated to see her as what Max Weber would call an "ideal type"—a complete and extreme example.

We tend to view gender as two fixed, binary roles. There are men and there are women. But in some parts of the world, it is not so rigidly binary. In Albania and parts of Afghanistan, for example, it was possible for a family lacking male heirs to make one of their daughters a "son" and treat her thereafter as a boy—and later a man. In Samoa, it is considered good luck to have child who is a Fa'afafine, or a boy who is somewhere between male and female. This third gender is definitely a male, but he also stays home and helps Mother with the housework, tends to the younger children, and nurtures the extended family (Anderson, 2011). The famous "ladyboys" of Thailand are, in a sense, a third gender; everyone knows they are biologically male, but they are treated and even exalted as women.

Judith Butler took our understanding of gender one step further by arguing that gender is fundamentally a "performance." Butler points out that "going drag" brings to light this nature. She writes, "Drag constitutes the mundane way in which genders are appropriated, theatricalized, worn, and done; it implies that all gendering is a kind of impersonation and approximation" (Butler, 1999, p. 580). Drag only makes sense to us, she is saying, because gender itself is a performance that involves some measure of costuming and dramatic architecting. Many women do this every day when they put on make-up; men do this when they attach a BlackBerry to their belt. Gender is not an *idée fixée*; its norms and ideals are fluid.

Marketers repeatedly make the mistake of equating "woman" with "someone who buys all the household commodities." As I once pointed out in a memo to a client, femininity is more akin to a role that a woman plays, not a fixed identity. Sometimes she takes on the entire role, and sometimes she picks and chooses aspects of the role she would like. This explains why a "busy mom" can also be a CEO, an investment banker, a soldier, a scientist, or anything else. Unfortunately, when we use the words "busy mom" to describe a woman, we conjure up the *role* of busy mom, and not actual women. Understanding how something like gender is a social construct is a huge advantage that ethnographers can bring to the private sector.

Using the lens of gender in private-sector ethnography means focusing on the process whereby individuals grapple with the "ideal" role of woman or man. For example, in one project I conducted on dessert food for a consumer packaged goods company, I pointed out that men between 28 and 45 were grappling with a shifting masculine role. These participants had new wives, young children, early careers, and big mortgages. The client wanted to see these men as teenaged boys, by feeding them messages that bordered on sexism. I pointed out that these men were coming to terms with their new responsibilities and did not respect men who were selfish, boyish and/or self-absorbed. Yet, they continued to pay homage to their "bachelor days" by engaging in symbolic competition and selfishness through "trash talk" and boys' nights. Their gender role was in flux, and they felt ambivalence about this. The right message here was to respect and celebrate their new selfless role as husband and father, thereby reinforcing the life change they were experiencing. At the same time, these men needed to feel that their "young self" was not shameful, but a source of fun. Given permission, these men would celebrate this young self, but were in the process of bidding it goodbye. Honoring this celebration was a more positive and uplifting message than stooping to sophomoric and sexist humor.

Economic Class

A second dynamic identity role we perform is that of economic class. As Oprah revealed very tellingly in her special on *Class in America*, most people identify themselves as "middle class" even when they are most obviously not. The role of "rich" or "poor" is one we also learn and one that changes. For this insight, we owe a debt to Karl Marx, whose greatest intellectual gift was to show that a person's economic power is not "naturally" endowed but a function of social conflict. In other words, wealth is not a "fact" but a socially constructed meaning that is debated, negotiated, and resisted. We battle for economic dominance beyond simply competing for dollars—we also compete for symbolic dominance. Pierre Bourdieu (1984) applied this concept to the very French notion of "taste." Accepting, as Marx does, that class identity is a function of social conflict, Bourdieu argued that we compete not just for actual fiscal capital but for what he called cultural capital. This kind of wealth is the "wealth" relating to knowledge about the "right" brands to buy. The "nouveaux riches" are not culturally wealthy, though they may have money. They lack cultural capital, not economic capital.

The Urban Hipster is the contemporary personification of cultural capital. She has very little money but exercises her knowledge of cool to exert her class dominance. Her capital is her knowledge of art shows, vintage clothing stores, little-known Italian bike designers, and, of course, "bands you haven't even heard of." The Hipster's "wealth" is not in her bank account; it is in her superior knowledge. She will use this knowledge to dominate others by restricting access to exclusive knowledge. She will not tell just anybody where she bought her vintage cowboy boots. She will nod at you knowingly if you somehow find your way to her favorite bar. She will sneer at those who do not have this knowledge. It is her way of exerting dominance, not with mere money, but with cultural know-how.

Most people working in business today almost never understand this insight. The luxury market is a case in point. Luxury goods are not simply a function of how much they cost, but the meanings that consumers ascribe to them. Goods that are expensive—but not exclusive—are not true luxury. The luxury market has grown in the last decade, leading to a degradation of both the quality and the exclusivity of goods (Thomas, 2008). Luxury is not simply a function of how much a good costs, but who has access to it. Those rich in cultural capital may not have money. Those with money may have no cultural capital. Marketers who seek those with large household incomes miss a very important nuance: people without cultural capital will actively reject goods they sense are "not for the likes of us." As Bourdieu explains, they "reject that which rejected them." A business owner who becomes successful may eschew that new Rolex because he believes it "for the rich." Sadly, the truly rich may also reject the Rolex because it is for the "nouveaux riches." For a Rolex to appeal to both groups, it must be both approachable and exclusive at the same time. This is a near impossibility. The error that many designers, marketers, and product managers make is to create an "upscale" product or experience. They don't realize they are actually actively alienating people who may very well have money to spend but who are uncomfortable with the symbols and trappings of refinement.

This is precisely where ethnographers can contribute to both product design and product marketing. Ethnographers have the ability to watch participants rejecting goods they consider "too fancy" or "too déclassé." Just as companies can make the mistake of creating products only "for the rich," they can err by making products modestly priced and widely available. The watch industry is an interesting case in point. Contrary to popular belief, many so-called "luxury" watches are rejected by the truly wealthy. In their survey of very wealthy people, the Luxury Institute found that the most popular watches among the rich were those made by Swiss watchmaker Franck Muller. The company makes fewer than 4,500 watches each year (Frank, 2007).

I once worked at a digital agency whose client was a luxury watch-maker. The creative team wanted to increase engagement among exist-ing and potential customers. Their idea was an online community. The account director asked me what I thought. I told him that if they really wanted to make the product "exclusive" that they should not give out "memberships" in this "club" to just anybody. It should be hard to "join." Just like Franck Muller, they should limit, not expand, access to the prod-uct. They should have secret activities and passwords to gain access to online and face-to-face events. This community would be impossible to join, he complained. Yes, I said, that is the point. In my research on trends in the luxury market, it was clear that there were too many products in the "mass luxury" segment, each battling hard to carve out a tiny slice of the lower-upper-class's preferences. In the end, the account team went another direction, but that luxury watchmaker continues to struggle to maintain its exclusive reputation as it expands its market share to include the "mass luxury" market. The "real" luxury market is now dominated by their competitors.

Race and Ethnicity

A third identity role that is relevant to private-sector ethnographers is race and ethnicity. Just like gender, we often conceive of race as a fixed binary category. You are either black or white. You are Jewish or Christian. But in reality, we face many instances where this is not as clear-cut. Recently, a Hungarian anti-Semitic politician was exposed as being, in fact, a Jew. He was expelled from his political party and disappeared from public view. Barack Obama identifies as black, even though his mother was visibly Caucasian. These incidents may reveal race and ethnicity as somewhat arbitrary, and that is because it *is* arbitrary.

Ironically, it is science itself that tells us race is largely a social fic-tion. Recent advances in DNA testing have shown us how difficult it is to define race biologically. Race is more of a social identity than it is a biological phenomenon.

It's particularly important for product managers to know how their products relate to "blackness" or "whiteness." Some products convey the "wrong" race for an individual consumer, one that she may wish to reject. Consider a fashion brand such as Ralph Lauren. This brand has a "preppy" history, evoking East Coast and Ivy League sensibility. Colors drawn from sailing, rowing, and other "white" sports are woven into the Lauren look. Imagine a black woman choosing this brand and what she grapples with in adopting it as her own. Terms like "oreo" suggest that there is a "correct" way to be black, and Ralph Lauren clothes may not fit that correct way. If a black woman's friends call her an "oreo," they are saying she is not displaying the "appropriate" amount of "blackness," as defined by them. Private-sector ethnographers know how seek to understand what this "appropriate" level is, whether it be for "blackness" or "whiteness," particularly for goods that convey symbolic capital. Racial identities are difficult for many people to portray, and products that project a narrow and simplistic notion of race can be rejected because of that simplicity.

Fitting Identities Together

We must also acknowledge that all three of these identity roles—gender, class and race—intersect. In the case of the black woman choosing Ralph Lauren, it means understanding that she is a woman, who performs certain feminine traits. She may also be an upper class individual who projects an upper-class "habitus" of exclusivity, refinement, and quiet reserve. Additionally, she is grappling with the identity of "blackness." Somehow, she must put together all of these roles at the same time. Sociologists call this process "intersectionality." A white woman who considers herself "middle class" must grapple with projecting the "appropriate" feminine, middle-class role that matches what others perceive her ethnicity to be. Marketers often fail to consider intersectionality in their strategies, in part because it is very complex to do so, but also because we tend to think in simple, binary categories. Private-sector ethnographers look for the struggles their participants experience in balancing their identities.

Theories of Social Context: Understanding Culture

Now that we know the ways in which individuals grapple with identity, we must also understand the context in which these identities play out. In some ways, this contextual focus is even more important for the ethnographer. The psychologist (particularly the social psychologist) focuses on the individual and his interactions with others, but it is the ethnographer that provides insight into the influences *culture* has on that individual. The factist approach puts *consumers* in the role of the expert because it assumes that consumers have "all the answers" about their social context. This creates the strange experience of consumers as the "experts" on culture, not the researcher. I have fielded many requests from market research managers to ensure that I ask participants for answers about social trends, without realizing that consumers are just as unaware of these trends as they are. As Malinowski points out, at times the individual himself may not be aware of his place in the overall cultural system; he may be acting out his role in relative ignorance of the wider social trends. It is the *ethnographer's* role to explain that system.

The word "culture" gets thrown around a lot in business today. Often people talk about "culture," but they rarely spell out what it means. In their report on innovation, for example, Booz & Company researched the "cultural" aspects of innovation in San Francisco (Jaruzelski, Le Merle, and Randolph, 2012). Yet they never define what culture actually is or how one can understand it, much less measure it. There is a distinct lack of clarity about what culture is and how it can be researched empirically.

We can operationalize culture as values, beliefs, and behaviors. This simple framework provides a very robust but also very clear roadmap for private-sector ethnographers.

Values

As Kluckhohn (1953) and Seeley (Seeley, Sim, and Loosely, 1956) have offered, value orientations fall along five axes:

1. Time orientation: What kind of time sense does this organization consider important? An exaltation of the past? A focus on the "now"? Or the focus on the future?

2. Activity: What kind of activity does this culture consider to be "correct"? Is being busy or active the "right" way of being? Is it preparing for the future or becoming? Or is it simply "being in the moment"?

3. Human relations: What is considered the right way to organize social life? Through competition? Collaboration? Hierarchy?

4. Human nature: What is humankind's "natural" way of being? Are we all born good, bad, or neutral?

5. Human-to-nature: How should humankind interact with nature? By dominating it? Living in harmony with it? Or by being submissive to it?

These values tend to cluster into like values. The notion that humans are born as inherently good jibes with a focus on the future, for example, while the idea that humans are born "bad" fits well with the idea that hierarchy is the best way to organize social relations.

This value framework reveals what a given culture considers important. In an organizational ethnography I completed, I used this framework to create a "value map" of two merging companies. Through interviews and observation, I discovered that the two companies had a "value gap" which would make the merger difficult to complete smoothly. Specifically, I noted that the purchasing company had a "collaborative" value orientation, while the purchased company had a "competitive" orientation. This conflict could be eased if the purchasing company allows continued competition, but creates new incentives for collaboration.

Figure 1: Value Orientation Model

	Activity	Time Orientation	Social Relations	Human to Nature	Human Nature
Aspirational Values	Becoming is best	Future oriented	Competitive	Humans dominate nature	Man is born good
Static Values	Just being is best	Present oriented	Collectivist	Humans in harmony with nature	Man is born neither good nor bad
Conservative Values	Being active is best	Past oriented	Hierarchical	Nature dominates humans	Man is born bad

Beliefs

What do consumers believe about a particular topic? Sunderland and Denny (2007) explain this quite clearly in their book, *Doing Anthropology in Consumer Research*. They suggest researchers ask simple questions about what they're researching—for example, what is "coffee"? Coffee is more than simply a brown drink, filtered from a bean. It is an experience.

It is a social event. It is an artisanal product. It is an excuse to meet. It is a love object. These are beliefs that consumers hold, though they may never have articulated them in these ways.

I applied this same rubric to a detailed ethnographic study of patients and physicians. Patients, I discovered, saw sickness as an "attack on the body." Implicitly, they believed the body was a "fortress" that could be protected with the right tools, such as ionic air purifiers, orange juice, and instant chicken soup! Physicians, on the other hand, talked about the body in mechanistic terms. They believed sickness to be an "error in the body's functioning." Implicitly, they subscribed to the biomedical model of illness, which has been well documented by many scholars (Agdal, 2005; McClain, 1977; Mykhalovskiy and Weir, 2004; Nettleton, 2006). This gap between patient perception and physician perception meant physician-oriented marketing materials were not right for patients. Patient marketing materials needed different metaphors for patients to understand them easily.

Understanding what consumers believe gives a coherent metaphor with which to build marketing or product design strategies. The product's design and marketing must match the ways in which consumers think about that product.

Behaviors

In his book, *The Study of Man* [sic], Linton (1936) offers a very simple and useful theoretical framework for studying behaviors. He argues that there are four types of behaviors: universals, specialties, alternatives, and peculiarities. Following Malinowksi here, Linton notes that people both follow rules and flout rules, and who does which when can tell us a great deal about a culture. Accordingly, universal behaviors aren't necessarily what everyone *does do*, but what everyone *should do*. In my example in Table 1, I show that wearing shoes is something that everyone should do in contemporary Western society. Some people wear certain types of shoes. That is, they engage in specialty behavior. For example, it is women who wear high heels. Specialties can reveal much about the symbolic hierarchy of a given social context. Perhaps only managers use a certain elevator, as was the case among senior General Motors executives, just before they were fired by their new boss, the U.S. government (Rattner, 2009).

Table 1: Linton's Conception of Behavior

Behavior	Description	Example
Universals	What everyone "should" do	Wear shoes
Specialties	What some roles (e.g., women, managers) do	Wear high heels, dress shoes
Alternatives	What some people do, within the realm of "personal taste" but not the ideal	Wear hot pink Doc Martins
Peculiarities	What only "strange" people do	Go barefoot

Alternatives are behaviors that are considered outside the norm, but within the realm of personal taste. This kind of behavior reveals much about the values of a given culture. A consumer may point to his neighbor's Christmas lights, still hanging outside in July, and say, "To each his own." But what he means is that this is not what one "ought" to do. His disapproval reflects the value of doing rather than being, for example. And finally, peculiarities are behaviors that would elicit curious stares or outright hostility. You may see this when a man wears a dress, when a stranger enters a home without knocking, or when a co-worker sleeps on top of her desk. These behaviors tell us what is considered not acceptable, and in turn, how that social context shapes individual behavior.

Back to the Truth

On that day when my professor Catherine used the word "verisimilitude," I, of course, immediately googled the definition of the word. Here is what I found.

Ver-i-si-mil-i-tude (noun).

1. the appearance of being true or real
2. something that only seems true

In other words, that old marketing adage, "perception is reality." Your job as a practical ethnographer is to discover that which appears true. What do consumers believe about this product? What do they say they do with this product? Ethnographers discover the perceptions of a product. They discover how people interpret that perception and how this product may—or may not—fit into their lives. Through this kind of lens, truth is what appears in everyday life. Ethnographers can help others in the private sector understand everyday truth, which is often hiding in plain sight.

Chapter 3
Managing a Private-Sector Ethnography Project

In the end, ethnographic project management is part Kabuki, part discipline. The key is knowing which parts are which. This chapter reveals "project management" as a series of mundane, but important, everyday rituals, that, when strung together, represent contemporary productivity as a tightly controlled, predictable practice, even when there is nothing predictable about it. Ethnographers can leverage their understanding of ritual to represent their craft as the quintessential project, even when it is actually nothing of the sort.

Corporate life brings a strange dissonance to ethnographic practice. Ethnographic work is often unstructured and iterative, while corporate processes are often highly structured. This contrast is almost immediately palpable to the ethnographer. I myself noticed this dissonance when I started a job as a research analyst in a digital agency. One of the first things I was trained to do as a research analyst was how to fill out an electronic time sheet. On my time sheet, I was to assign my work time to a "project," which was assigned to a particular client. I found this surprising, annoying, and even a bit strange. I had been out of the corporate sector for almost three years. I had worked in non-profit and academic institutions during that time, but I had lost touch with the cultural "know

Practical Ethnography: A Guide to Doing Ethnography in the Private Sector by Sam Ladner, 39–54. © 2014 Left Coast Press, Inc. All rights reserved.

how" of the corporate world. As I would soon learn, accounting for time is *de rigueur* in consultancies of many types. From advertising to law to construction, every moment of every workday is accounted for—even if that accounting is incorrect. The actual numbers are not important, I learned, but the *spirit of accounting for time* is a key feature of contemporary private-sector practice.

Being a private-sector ethnographer means working within this context, even though ethnography as a method is not temporally organized in the same way. Ethnographic work, as I showed in Chapter 1, is usually considered an all-consuming, solitary, and above all, *long* pursuit. It involves a "series of friendly conversations" (Spradley, 1979) which do not fit neatly into electronic time sheets. Ethnographers have demonstrated again and again that their best laid plans have been thrown out the window once fieldwork begins (Briggs, 1970; Fine, 1993; Seeley, Sim, and Loosely, 1956). How can a private-sector ethnographer navigate contemporary corporate life when her chosen research method continually conflicts with its time regime?

In this chapter, I will again describe the contemporary corporate world through a cultural lens, with a particular emphasis on how work is temporally organized. I will then describe how to organize and manage a typical ethnographic project in the private sector. I will lay out the basic steps to a private-sector ethnography project, as well as how these steps are taken up and enacted in contemporary corporate practice. You'll see the cultural touchstones of "good" project management, which will help you adapt your methods to be successful in the typical private-sector organization. I will outline how and in what ways private-sector ethnographers can avoid having this temporal context negatively affect the outcomes of their research. I will offer practical, step-by-step advice on how to organize and, perhaps more important, represent your ethnographic research project to your clients and stakeholders.

The Temporal Landscape of Today's Corporation

Life in today's corporate world plays out alongside a frenetic, 24/7 drumbeat. This is due in part to globalization, which has increased competition and "annihilated" time zones (Castells, 1996; Laxer, 1995). Running a global business means operating continuously, according to the timekeeping of the entire world, and not just one's local market. Today's typical corporation operates in a constant state of perceived[1] time-scarcity which, when coupled with extensive technology use, leads to ever fewer unstructured minutes and hours. Glenday (2011) calls this unstructured temporal rubric "loose time," which is emergent and often creative. By contrast, he notes, "taut time" is organized according to schedule and designed specifically. "Loose time" is now somewhat of an anomaly; "taut time," which is structured and organized, is more the norm. Children's play, for example, was once a rich cultural experience created and governed by children themselves; today, children's activities are tightly choreographed by adults (Gray, 2011). Academia is also subject to this shift. Academics struggle with the growing prevalence of taut time (Menzies and Newson, 2007), with increasing amounts of committee work and the never-ending flow of email. Ethnography was born in academia, which was once fully organized according to loose time. It was once more common for academics to have wide swaths of loose time, and this continues to be the ideal way in which to do research. Academic ethnographers today struggle to fit ethnography's typically long timelines into the increased tempo of everyday academic life (Trotter, Needle, Goosby, Bates, and Singer, 2001).

In the private sector, the loose time temporal rhythm is especially discordant. Culturally, it is expected that we account for time somehow; the content of that accounting is, in some ways, irrelevant (Ladner, 2008). Even in organizations that sell products (as opposed to selling their time to other companies), the symbolic act of accounting for time is infused into everyday life. Accounting for time is the enactment of "time thrift," which, for professionals who sell their time, is the symbolic act of hoarding resources. In a sense, accounting for time is the contemporary act of accumulation of capital (Ladner, 2008). Benjamin Franklin famously remarked, "Time is money." In today's corporation, accounting for time is the accompanying practice.

The "project" is a natural outcome of this temporal landscape. The early 20th century gave us F. W. Taylor and his "scientific management," or "Taylorism," which assumes there is "one best way" to do everything (Rinehart and Faber, 1987). Today's corporate touchstone is the "project." A project is the temporary organization of people marshaled around a shared goal (Lundin and Soderholm, 1995). The primary goal of a project is to *create something* within a *discrete period of time* (Boltanski and Chiapello, 2005). The assumption here is that for a thing to come into existence, it requires concerted governance, particularly over how time is spent. Having no such governance is antithetical to contemporary corporate life. It is, of course, a bit absurd when you think of all the things that have come into existence, long before there was any such thing as a "project." Some of humanity's greatest achievements were created without the benefit of a project plan. Yet, today there is an assumption that time governance is required for anything to be created. Ethnographic research projects are no exception—it is now expected that to produce anything, one must budget for time, account for that time, and allocate that time to particular people in a particular order.

Thus came the discipline of "project management," which is now arguably the profession most emblematic of this new age (Muzio, Hodgson, Faulconbridge, Beaverstock, and Hall, 2011). "Project management" is typically interpreted as the control of both people and time, and is usually a deeply positivistic endeavor (Pollack, 2007). While project managers are often tasked with very "human" activities such as communication and reaching consensus, project management as a discipline typically operates in a quasi-scientific manner, with the diligent collection and analysis of data that are mostly quantitative and mostly related to time and effort.

Given ethnography's interpretivist standpoint, the very notion of accounting for time seems foreign and even threatening. Ethnography is often ambiguous, rapidly changing, and unpredictable. By contrast, project managers are trained to manage discrete tasks in a sequential manner. Even though this approach often leads to project failures, the dominant paradigm of project management is positivist and rigid. Rigid schedules and the inability to change direction have frequently led to failed projects, yet project management remains largely unchanged in its practices (Pollack, 2007). How can ethnographers fit within this rigid framework? In the remainder of this chapter, I will show how ethnographers can represent themselves as culturally competent members of the corporation, without sacrificing the need for adaptability and participant-led research.

The ethnographer need not abandon her participants' standpoint in order to please her clients, but she must first realize that there is a cultural gap between the participants and the clients.

Principles for Being an Interpretivist Project Manager

My first large ethnography project as an independent researcher was deeply intimidating. I had landed a large, respected client who was willing to pay good money for the expertise of my assembled team and me. I had spent a fair bit of time convincing my main client stakeholder to fund the project, and when the green light finally went on, I realized I had to show her that I could be trusted. I had every faith that I could do the project well. The two ethnographers that I hired were both highly trained sociologists who had done similar observational work before. I myself had done dozens of these projects already and was not at all concerned about my ability to deliver insight. What I was concerned about was convincing my client that I could organize and run the project. I realized that I needed some principles for managing the project that did not compromise my emic commitment. I would be an interpretivist project manager.

An "interpretivist project manager" is someone who sees and understands the gap between her interpretivist method (in this case, ethnography) and the positivist bent of her clients and stakeholders. The interpretivist project manager sees the act of "project management" itself as a product of culture, one that is socially constructed and infused with meaning. An interpretivist project manager does not mindlessly adopt positivist project-management techniques, but instead reflects on their cultural purpose and employs them critically. Her job is to understand the positivist standpoint, empathize with it, and make her standpoint more intelligible to her clients. The secret to conducting a fruitful and enlightening ethnography in the private sector, then, is to recognize the temporal landscape, pay heed to its cultural practices of accounting for time, while simultaneously preparing clients and stakeholders for inevitable surprises. As a private-sector ethnographer, you are an interpretivist stranger in a foreign positivist land. Your job is to establish trust by creating a time budget but to also have the courage to break that time budget when fieldwork demands it. Being an interpretivist project manager will allow you to conduct business in the "appropriate" fashion, but will also allow you flexibility and an emic standpoint in your research.

One final aspect to being an interpretivist project manager is recognizing the ritualistic nature of project management. There is a cadence and a rhythm to managing a project. Regularity breeds familiarity; members of the project team will appreciate the regularity and the dramatization of key project milestones. Ethnographers study ritual, but surprisingly are often terrible at designing it. Project management is a mundane set of practices that can be emulated and adapted with a drop of dramatic flourish to cast the ethnographic project as a satisfying narrative.

Estimating the Cost of a Private-Sector Ethnography Project

The first step in starting an ethnography in the private sector is to create the rough project plan, in the form of a proposal to your clients or stakeholders. This means breaking down each successive task in the typical project, assigning a time budget and people to that task, and totaling up the entire projected cost. This is the process of creating what looks to be taut time, but in reality is simply the process of cultural assimilation; project plans symbolically convey the shared value of taut time to your clients and stakeholders. Ethnography is typically a time-based billing structure and, like all time-based billing services, faces the problem of being "too fast." Do not be afraid to set high hourly rates to compensate for your years of experience and training. Better yet, use a per diem rate and never allow for less than half a day's billing. Remember that the project proposal is an *estimate*, not a bill. You must also keep track of your time throughout the length of the project and ensure that you are not going "over budget" in terms of time (more about that later).

When you produce a professional project plan, you are demonstrating that you understand contemporary corporate practice. Building a project plan is surprisingly easy to do with today's software. Below is a typical task list for a private-sector ethnography project. I exported this directly from my project management software called OmniPlan (Microsoft Project will also do the trick, as will Merlin). I typically write up the project proposal using this software and then never use it again throughout the project. Its job is to show my client that I have thought

Table 2: Private Sector Ethnography Sample Project Plan

	Approximate Duration	People Involved
1. Planning	**2 weeks**	
a. Planning for kick-off meeting	1d	Ethnographer
b. On-site kick-off meeting	1d	Ethnographer
c. Research and sampling design	1w	Ethnographer
d. Interview and observation guide	1w 0.25h	Ethnographer
e. Recruitment screener	2d	Ethnographer
2. Insight Collection	**3 weeks**	
a. Recruitment	2w	Recruiter; ethnographer
b. Ethnographic interviews	1w 1d	Ethnographer; client or stakeholder
3. Analysis	**1–2 weeks**	
a. On-site collaborative analysis	4h	Ethnographer; client or stakeholder
b. Report document preparation	1w 1d	Ethnographer
4. Applying insights	**1–2 days**	
a. Report presentation	4h	Ethnographer; client or stakeholder
b. Insight brainstorming session	4h	Client or stakeholder; ethnographer
Total	**6 to 7 weeks**	

deeply about the tasks involved, how long they will take, who will do them, and how much the project will cost.

This framework is the general project outline I work with routinely. I start with this skeleton outline, and add or subtract tasks as needed for each individual project. Some projects require less client involvement. Some projects have smaller budgets or timelines, so a few steps must be pared down or skipped altogether. Some projects take longer due to more specific recruitment criteria, some take longer because of a shortage of staff. Delivering the "report" can mean producing several different types of documents. As I will describe later, it may be an old-fashioned Word document, a PowerPoint presentation, a video documentary, or even a podcast. This outline is typical for private sector ethnography.

Those trained in academic ethnography will note that there are many, many things missing from this project outline. Namely, the literature review, the transcription of interview audio tapes, the qualitative coding in NVivo or similar analysis, and the iteration of moving from theory to the field, and back to theory once again. For the academically trained ethnographer, simply looking at this project outline can seem threatening because it drastically underestimates the time and expertise required to garner true insight.

But remember: you are an interpretivist stranger in a positivist land. This outline is not "the project" but the positivist *representation* of that project. You are designing this project outline not to specifically outline every task involved with ethnography, but to show to your clients and stakeholders that you are aware that time governance is both important and possible. You can use this project outline to estimate your time, provide a budget, and above all, to show that you are familiar with project management as a discipline.

Bronislaw Malinowski would likely never secure a private-sector ethnography project today because he would be culturally unaware of these contemporary practices. Many current academic ethnographers are likely in the same boat; they would be unable to communicate in terms of time budgets, sequential tasks, and people involved. But private-sector ethnographers must be able to communicate their project in these terms.

As you can see, the typical ethnographic project requires far more expertise than is readily apparent to the client. If you do not have an advanced social science degree, it will take you longer to formulate a solid research design, including good research questions and a clear set of objectives. If you lack private-sector experience, it will take you longer to manage client needs. Both of these invisible tasks are key to making a realistic ethnographic project plan.

Assembling the Team

In Hollywood, film and television "projects" typically involve an initial stage of assembling a highly skilled creative team. Most of the work implicit in this stage is the maintenance of loose, professional networks of people. Indeed, the major "off-season" task of those in film and television is keeping in touch with former professional contacts (Randle and Culkin, 2009). Ethnography is often similar in that it involves the assembly of a team that ideally has worked together previously. Before projects even begin, the skilled ethnographer knows to whom she can turn for a particular skill set. This means developing and maintaining relationships with research recruiters, designers and illustrators, and perhaps most importantly, other ethnographers.

Unfortunately, the research "team" is oftentimes a single person. I have done dozens of ethnography projects and have only been lucky enough to work with anyone for a handful of those. But I have learned that recruiting participants is by far the most labor-intensive stage of the research project. For that reason, I usually factor in the cost of a professional recruitment company, or at the very least, an assistant who can book participants' time. Recruitment is one of the few tasks in this kind of project that does not require specialized knowledge. For this reason, I usually take this one task off my plate, and make sure I stay in touch with people who are very good at it.

In addition to a recruiter the typical research team includes a primary ethnographer, a research assistant to take notes, record video, and/or snap still photos. This assistant is a "nice to have" addition to the project, and is often the first cost to be cut when budgets get tight.

Managing the Project

In his ethnography of an Australian hotel, Bunzel (2002) discovered that the senior staff gathered regularly to discuss the hotel's functioning. Directors of each department would make brief announcements about "the numbers," but critically, few had any idea what their colleagues' numbers actually meant. The head of catering didn't know the significance of how many rooms were cleaned by housekeeping. Likewise, the head of housekeeping didn't know the significance of how many meals were served. As Bunzel points out, "the numbers" themselves were not the issue; it was how work tempo was communicated *through the numbers* that mattered. The head of housekeeping may infer that business has slowed down because of the decrease in the number of meals. The head of catering may not know that the housekeeping staff is spread too thin because the number of rooms cleaned rose and no new staff was added. The head of reception may infer by the other directors' tone and urgency that guests are not satisfied with current service levels. The ritual of symbolically "gathering around the numbers" every week symbolized how the hotel, like other contemporary organizations, was "projectified" (Muzio et al., 2011). Ethnographers may note this kind of ritual signifies an attempt to control time and space, an ideal emblematic of contemporary Western culture.

Managers of ethnography projects must also adopt the ritualistic "gathering around the numbers." This ritual provides clients and stakeholders a reassurance that work is "getting done," even if they do not understand the significance of "the numbers." The manager of an ethnography must communicate how much work has been produced, and if this is above or below expectations. Ethnographers are not typically in the business of operationationalizing their interpretive work into quantitative indicators, but by doing so, you are speaking the language of the positivism, and thereby providing reassurance. What indicators should an ethnographer communicate? In a private-sector ethnography project, "the numbers" could include:

1. Time
   a. How much time is left in the overall time budget?
   b. Do we have enough time allotted to finish the project on time?
2. Overall tasks
   a. How many tasks have been completed?
3. Fieldwork
   a. How many participants have been recruited?
   b. How many field visits have been completed?
   c. How many participants have been interviewed?
   d. How many incidental participants (for example, co-workers, family members) have been interviewed?
4. Fieldwork and analysis
   a. How many field notes have been written up?
   b. How many analytic memos have been written up?
   c. How many photographs have been taken?
   d. How many hours of observation have taken place?
   e. How many minutes/hours of video have been shot?
5. Final report
   a. How much of the final report/documentary/presentation has been completed?
   b. How many stakeholders have weighed in on the initial findings?
   c. How many stakeholders have been presented with the final findings?
6. Outcomes
   a. How many actions have been initiated, based on the findings?

Using these indicators in regular project meetings will show your clients and stakeholders that your project is within the realm of contemporary practice.

Crucially, ethnographers must also set a benchmark for what is "normal" in ethnographic practice. Clients, particularly those unfamiliar with the method, will look to the ethnographer for guidance as to whether these numbers are good or bad. It's good practice, therefore, to keep records of these benchmarks across projects. Are you tracking above or below what would typically be expected? The key indicator should always be the time remaining in the project. If 80 percent of the work is done and 50 percent of the time allotted remains, the project is in good shape. If 20 percent of the work is done and 20 percent of the allotted time remains, the project is in trouble. But with regular check-ins, this kind of time crisis should never come as a surprise.

But—and this is a very large but—ethnographers should never forget that the method itself is not designed for this rigid projectification. It was designed to be a deep, immersive experience that transforms its practitioners' mindsets. The goal is never to achieve "the numbers," but to achieve the *explanation* of your participants' cultural practices. In order to get to that explanation, you must assure your clients and stakeholders that the project meets the contemporary minimum requirements of what a "project" is culturally understood to be.

When Things Go Wrong

One of the major problems I have encountered with private-sector ethnography is that clients expect it to be "flaky." By this, I mean that clients expect ethnographers to be out of touch with the fast-paced, work-focused tempo of business life. I had one client express relief that I was not a "crazy cat lady" (even though I do own a cat). Because interpretivist methods are unfamiliar to most of them, clients expect ethnography not to comply with their projectification of everyday life. You may find there are stakeholders in the wider organization that are hoping for the project to fail because they subscribe to another form of truth or validity. One way their suspicions are confirmed is when the ethnography fails to produce results in a given period of time.

Unfortunately, this often happens in ethnography. Anyone who has done any field-based research will know that sometimes things do not go as planned. There are minor catastrophes like taciturn participants, participants who don't engage in the practice you're researching, or homes or offices unwelcoming to an ethnographer. Some of us even have stories of major catastrophes like participants kicking us out of those homes or offices! If there is one thing to remember about managing an ethnography project, it is that your carefully laid project plan is just that: a plan. It is not the way the project will work out.

What if things go wrong? What if you get the wrong participants, or not enough participants? Remember that you have built trust with your clients and stakeholders by diligently budgeting for time, accounting for time spent, and duly "gathering around the numbers." If things go wrong, you have already bought yourself a great deal of credibility as an interpretivist stranger in a positivist land. Your job now is to mitigate the impact of the negative events by stealing time from another task. Since you have budgeted and accounted for time, you can tell your client exactly how much time you are going to "take" from the collaborative analysis session, or from the preparation of the report. You may end up with too few participants, in which case you will have "the gift of time" to devote to deeper analysis or more time on-site with the client after the report is delivered.

The secret to dealing with small and major catastrophes is to prepare yourself and your client about their inevitability. Then, even if things do go wrong, your "projectification" of ethnography has been above reproach. Again, regular check-ins are critical in achieving this ideal. It also helps if the budget has a bit of padding in terms of time; no client ever complained when a project was delivered early. Another way to prepare clients for potential deviations from the "official" project plan is simply to tell them early and often that it is normal to change direction in the middle of an ethnography. Many clients are accustomed to traditional market-research projects, which oftentimes go strictly according to plan. Educating clients up front about ethnography's inherent unpredictability will go a long way, should things go south.

Delivering the Project

Once you have completed the fieldwork and analysis and prepared your report (in whatever form it is in), you must deliver the project. Project delivery in the projectified world is a particular type of ritual. Suppliers prepare a "deliverable" (a Word document, a PowerPoint presentation), and confer with their direct client over its content. The client will be the person whom insiders associate with the ethnography itself. For this reason, his approval is incredibly important. Private-sector ethnographers must fight their urge to claim expert privilege over the entire contents of the "deliverable" because they will not have to defend its contents in the future. It is the client that will have to do this to his superiors and colleagues. Delivery, then, involves the client giving the deliverable a tone and cadence that is culturally resonant and acceptable.

I once had a colleague who had completed a freelance ethnography for a design firm. She was very pleased with her research but was deeply dismayed to see the final report, which contained made-up quotes from participants. She called me to talk about what she should do. It turns out that the manager at the design firm had no clear understanding what symbolic violence he had committed by changing participants' quotes. As far as he was concerned, the spirit was more or less the same, so what was the big deal? My colleague was aghast, and understandably so. She and I discussed the problem culturally. The real problem was that the design manager was ignorant of the values of ethnographic research, which include an emic perspective. He did not intend to offend my anthropologist colleague, but he managed to do perhaps the most offensive thing possible. She and I discussed what could be done. First, we decided she should tell him what the "emic perspective" is, why it matters, and what his actions signaled. Then, she would suggest ways to re-write the report to mirror authentically the experiences of the participants, without compromising clarity in the report. If direct quotes weren't "powerful" enough, she would offer snippets from her field notes.

What this anecdote reveals is that report delivery is where many academically trained ethnographers find themselves derailed. What they must realize is that there are different values in the private sector, which may result in deeply offensive actions that are not intended to be so.

Finally, report delivery is also a ritual, in the Durkheimian sense of the word, meaning it marks a temporal milestone we often consider "the end." Durkheim's catalogue of religious practices demonstrates that theatrical delivery is a key aspect to marking time. Even Hollywood has the much vaunted "wrap party" designed to punctuate "the end" of the project (and, conveniently, to create opportunities to cement professional relationships for the next project). Ironically, ethnographers often forget to dramatize the presentation of their findings, despite being deeply familiar with the symbolic importance of ritual itself. Present your findings in a fashion befitting this dramatic moment. Do not agree to a teleconference. Do not simply email your report. Instead, create an event with ritualistic flourishes that befits the insights you have gathered. This could simply be a face-to-face meeting with a presentation that provides a build-up, inciting action, a climax, and a denouement.

Reviewing the Project

There is a tradition in many companies, from technology to media, to conduct a "post mortem" on completed projects. Software companies may do this after a product has shipped and newspapers may do this the morning after the newspaper was printed. The goal of the post mortem is to review the project, identify its successes and failures, and attempt to make institutional changes to ensure successes continue and failures are not repeated.

Ethnography projects can garner great benefit from the post mortem. Consider some of the typical successes an ethnography can have: transformed client mindset, an overarching mental model for the product, deep insight into customers' mind sets, metaphors for design, and so forth. But there are just as likely a list of failures that can come from ethnography. From my own experience, this list includes some of the most common private-sector ethnography failures: poor recruiting, not enough participants, shallow insight, findings that aren't actionable, client dissatisfaction, lack of impact in the client organization, misunderstanding of the project goals by clients.

To effectively review your project, add the post mortem to your initial project plan. It's ideal if you can involve the client in this process, but if you cannot, it is still worthwhile. All team members should attend. If it's a team of one, then conduct the post mortem as a writing process. You can follow this very simple process:

What worked on this project?

What didn't work in this project?

What was missing from this project?

Answering these questions, however briefly, will give you and your team an opportunity to consider how to improve later projects. Conduct the post mortem no later than one week following delivery of the final report, otherwise important details will be forgotten or lost. Capture the outcomes from the post mortem in a shared document that can be viewed, edited, and updated. And most importantly, review this document prior to each new engagement. Have you fixed what went wrong? Have you added the needed resources? Can you emulate the same successes?

Strong private-sector ethnographers know that projects do require some positivist oversight, but that this oversight can pull the project away from its original intention. Interpretivist project managers aim to uncover deep, emic understanding of their participants. If the project management rubric prevents this process, it must be insulated from the actual work. Its representation may be the ticket to gaining client acceptance, but it must be held separate from the original goal.

Chapter 4
Ethnographic Tools

I love to watch home improvement shows. My favorite is *Holmes on Homes*, starring Mike Holmes, veteran contractor and probable obsessive compulsive. The show starts with Mike coming into a home that has been somehow desecrated by an ill-trained, lazy, or even malicious fellow contractor. Mike gets a tour from the homeowners, then returns on his own and does a deeper inspection. He then ceremoniously gathers the homeowners for the bad news. How badly did this contractor treat you? Very badly. How deeply flawed is your house? Very deeply. How am I going to fix it? I'm going to "do it right." The homeowners' eyes often fill with tears of relief, and Mike gets to work forthwith.

One of my favorite parts of the show is where Mike gives a detailed overview of a new tool or "product" he's using to fix the home. Let's say the homeowners' bathroom is in rough shape. He will show the camera the watertight liner his team is going to use on the floor underneath the tiles. He goes into great detail on how this product is a vast improvement over the one the homeowner previously had. But the best part is that Mike doesn't stop there. He goes into excruciating detail on how to properly install the product, the typical rookie mistakes that novice contractors make, and the cheap shortcuts malicious ones make. He will often look into the camera and sternly warn the viewer to watch out for these mistakes and cheap tricks. For Mike, craftsmanship matters.

Practical Ethnography: A Guide to Doing Ethnography in the Private Sector by Sam Ladner, 55–68. © 2014 Left Coast Press, Inc. All rights reserved.

This chapter takes a page from Mike Holmes. I will show you the vast array of new tools that are available for ethnographers, and give an honest evaluation of why they are better than older tools. But just like Mike, I will show you how ethnographic craftsmanship is a critical component to this process. I will warn you away from rookie mistakes, and hopefully convince you to avoid cheap tricks. Unlike Mike, however, I bring a self-reflective eye to the normative nature of these tools and the dreaded concept of "best practices."

Watching Mike Holmes always makes me feel inadequate and vaguely anxious. I tend to look around our home and notice all the rookie mistakes we've made, and feel angry at the cheap tricks committed by contractors we've hired. My house looks less than perfect and deserving of some Holmes-like OCD. But then I remember that I'm a sociologist. I remember that there is such a thing as normativity or what I "should" do with my home. I relax a bit when I reflect on the reality of my own life, with my own priorities, which are very different than Mike Holmes's priorities. Likewise, I invite you to reflect on the tools I review here and consider your own ethnographic practice. Your priorities are different than mine, or any other ethnographer's. Consider which "rookie mistakes" you are willing to accept and which you are not. Cracks in your practice are not only acceptable, they are unavoidable. Reflect upon your own goals as you read this chapter, and adopt the tools that best suit them.

Types of Tools

Ethnographic practice has come a long way since Margaret Mead shot 22,000 rolls of film on the island of Samoa. Contemporary ethnographers can use a vast array of digital tools to help them collect, analyze, and report ethnographic findings. These digital tools increase your speed as a researcher, allow you to make connections more easily, and help you report your findings more meaningfully to your clients and stakeholders. But what none of these new tools does is make you a better ethnographer! Just like new bathroom liners don't make poor contractors better, digital tools will never improve your ability to interview, analyze, or synthesize. They will do what computers have always done: alleviate you from mundane, repetitive tasks. As philosopher Hubert Dreyfus (1992) tells us, computers still cannot think themselves, but they can *help us think*. This is your rule of thumb for using ethnographic tools: let computers do mundane, repetitive tasks that require vigilance and precision. Your mind is very bad at such tasks. Instead, make the digital tools calculate, count, navigate, and sift. Your job is to do what human minds do exceedingly well: pattern recognition, synthesis, leaps of abductive logic. This chapter will focus on what tools can do for you, and Chapter 9 on analysis will focus on what you should be doing with your amazing human mind.

Veteran private-sector ethnographers do something unique: they think qualitatively differently than new ethnographers. Progressing from novice to master involves seeing things in an entirely new way. We are not just faster; we are better. As Hubert Dreyfus and his brother Stuart tell us elsewhere (2008) the difference between competence and mastery is that masters are able to quickly discern the nature of the problem at hand and swiftly bring to mind several potential solutions to that problem. Just as quickly, the master then selects the right solution for the problem. The leap from competence to mastery is not a function of faster brain processing, but of faster pattern recognition; the higher order thinking of a master ethnographer relies on his ability to consider—and dismiss—potential paths without actually going through an itemized list of pros and cons.[1] Sadly, there are no tools that will transform you from a novice to a competent, much less to a master. But there are ways you can construct your tools to help you recognize patterns more quickly. In the rest of this chapter, I will provide an overview of tools you can use in every stage of the ethnographic project.

Research Design Tools: Reviewing Past Knowledge

In this phase of research, you are considering the nature of the problem at hand. What do my clients need to know? How can ethnography help them learn that? What is the general topic area, and how can I turn that into a research question? What kinds of things should we observe in the field? What should we ask participants? What are my timelines? What is my budget?

The tools that most help you manage your past knowledge and quickly sift through potential solutions to the problem at hand. Sociologist C. Wright Mills famously (1959) called this process going through your "files." Sociologists should spend time periodically going through the scraps of interesting insights they have captured from magazines, books, newspapers, and journal articles, Mills argued, so that they may make new cognitive connections (not to mention so that they can throw out all that extra paper!). As you sift through your "files," allow the computer to remember the exact citation or keyword. Your job is to synthesize and make connections that the computer cannot. The citation manager is an invaluable tool in this phase. Citation management tools like Endnote, Zotero, and Mendeley help organize academic and applied papers, reports, journal articles, and books that researchers build and maintain as a way of managing their knowledge. They allow their users to import and annotate the papers themselves. Users can also tag individual citations with their own keywords such as "research design," for example, or "user experience." I started using Endnote when completing my master's degree. An older PhD student once recommended it to me, and thankfully, I took her advice. Since then I've started using Mendeley, which is a cloud-based service that allows you to connect to other researchers and browse their databases. Crucially, these tools help you insert citations and automatically generate bibliographies, which is an invaluable function in the academic world. It comes in handy in the private sector as well when you need to show exactly where you got a statistic or concept. But generally in the private sector, citations are less relevant, so private sector ethnographers can use the databases to keyword search and quickly isolate past studies of interest. Consider them a personal knowledge management system, rather than a citation manager.

Private-sector ethnographers must also manage the knowledge they themselves create through their own research. This means having a good personal knowledge management strategy for all past research projects. For this purpose, digital data capturing software is incredibly helpful. Digital data capturing software is a vast improvement over our usual ways of knowledge management. Many of us use email as our primary knowledge management tool. Gwidzka (2004) calls these people the "keepers," who find comfort in keeping information in email format. But we know that this kind of management style has large labor costs; you will spend more time looking for your information if you store it in email instead of in other file formats (Conrow, 2010).[2] Searching your computer or using an email-based knowledge management system is what most people actually do, but it doesn't put the computer to work for you, and you still have to do much of the manual labor.

Digital data capturing tools allow you to keep unstructured notes, images, screen captures, and web pages in a single place. Digital capturing tools include Evernote, OneNote, and Google Keep. Evernote is a cloud-based system that allows you to capture web pages, personal notes, photos, audio and video files into individual "notes," which you can then organize into separate notebooks. As with citation managers, you can tag each note entry with keywords that are relevant to you, such as "fieldnotes" or "analytic memos" or "client requirements." OneNote for Windows has similar functionality and is integrated directly into Microsoft Office, so that you can share with other members of your team, as well as store in the cloud, if you wish. Google Keep does the same kind of integration for Google-based documents. If you are the kind of person who receives, generates, and uses a lot of paper, you may wish to use a tool like Shoeboxed, which is a cloud based service that scans your paper receipts or documents. Just mail them an envelope of paper, and within two weeks, you will have all those papers scanned and available through their web interface. This may be useful for people who collect paper artifacts, but it is really intended to keep track of receipts and bills.

In short, the research design phase is one in which the ethnographer is sifting through old knowledge to apply it to a new, given problem. The master ethnographer has a deep, almost unconscious, connection to this old knowledge, but the novice can use these digital tools to improve her practice. The key is not good knowledge management, though that definitely helps. The important process here is making those cognitive connections by regularly poring through and thinking about disparate sources of knowledge. Once that becomes somewhat embedded within an ethnographer's mind, the research design process definitely proceeds more quickly.[3]

Recruitment Tools: Reaching Out and Keeping Track

During the recruitment phase, the ethnographer's main task is to gain access to qualified participants. This stage is particularly difficult in the private sector because the general population is relatively unfamiliar with the *in situ* method of ethnography. Ask an average person, "What is a focus group?" and he or she would like give you an accurate answer. Ask that same person, "What is ethnography?" and perhaps more crucially, "Would you participate in one?" and you are likely to get blank stares and perhaps even hostile looks. As such, recruiting for private-sector ethnography is labor-intensive and should be managed closely by the researcher. Tools that help in this phase are similar to the research design phase in that they allow the ethnographer quick access to useful information. But unlike in the research design phase, recruitment requires the ethnographer to make connections with real people. Accordingly, social media can usually enhance recruitment.

I personally have outsourced much of my recruitment. As I mentioned earlier, recruitment is one of the few tasks that does not require ethnographic skill to be done well, so it is one of the few tasks that can be outsourced to a third party or a research assistant without compromising the overall quality of the study. But in order for participants to even know about your project, you will need to have what I call a "digital homestead." By this I mean that you must stake out some space on the web that allows people to forward and trade information about your project. It must be easily shared with others. I have seen many academic ethnographers produce "flyers" or PDF documents that can be emailed but cannot be shared via Facebook or Twitter because they do not have a web location. People who know potential participants may not know these participants' email addresses, but are connected to them in some other way. It's critical that you accommodate these non-mail networks. Have at least a single web page with some cursory information about the project and contact information. This allows your project to be sent throughout your wider social network without the use of email. Note that some social networks can offer you a digital homestead, but their sharing and privacy settings may make it difficult to share the page easily with those not on those networks. That's why it's ideal to have a web page that you yourself control.

The primary tool for recruitment, then, is a digital homestead. This can be a blog set up using a free tool such as Wordpress, or it can be a page on your own web site. It can even be an open Google spreadsheet or document. The only important aspect is that it is open to anyone who would like to see it (this is why I don't advise making only a Facebook page; many people do not use Facebook and may not have access to a Facebook page). The digital homestead's purpose is simply to have a single, accessible location to tell people about the project. Note that here I do not talk about sampling methods, which are surely germane to this phase of research. Consider reading about that in Chapter 7, "Sampling."

The second major task in recruitment is to manage appointments. There are many digital tools that allow people to create and share appointments, yet I am stunned at how infrequently people use them. Consider one of my favorite recruitment companies, God bless them, that uses an Excel spreadsheet, emailed to me multiple times over the course of the project. Each email contains a spreadsheet, named exactly the same as the previous version, but with new information added. There is no way to quickly scan and see when and where appointments have been booked, not to mention the fact that you're constantly sifting through your emails to find the most recent version! Talk about version control! Instead of using a document or spreadsheet, consider digital calendaring options which can be shared with your recruiters or research assistants and any other team members you have. A Google Calendar or Outlook 365 calendar can be shared with anyone, because it lives on the web. This makes it possible for your recruiters to book appointments in times that suit you. Alternatively, you could use an appointment-finding tool, such as Doodle, which allows several people to vote on the best time for a shared appointment. This could even be shared directly with potential participants, if your project suits that approach.

A third task in this phase is managing participant information. In this phase, a spreadsheet is definitely the best tool to use because it will discipline you into creating categories, or even variables, to describe your participants. You can record their addresses and names, as well as their recruitment criteria, such as the type of product or service they use, or their occupation. Starting to describe your participants like this in the beginning stages of the project sets you on the path of summarizing early, which is a critical task later on in analysis. Keep that participant spreadsheet and expand upon it throughout the project. It will come in handy.

Fieldwork Tools: Collecting and Archiving

Fieldwork is all about collecting data. This means your tools need to help you collect, and later to synthesize, information about your participants. Again, much has changed since Margaret Mead's time. Digital collection tools go beyond simply recording interactions; they allow you to store and tag interactions for future use. They also allow you to share these data easily with other members of the research team and your clients. Unlike survey research, however, the ethnographer himself is the instrument for data collection. Unsurprisingly, tools become a very personal thing. Ethnographers often prefer to develop their own personalized set of tools. Below is a description of some contemporary tools that you may wish to integrate into your practice.

In my standard "fieldwork kit," I include three items: a digital camera, my Livescribe pen, a notebook, and my smartphone. I add other items from time to time, but any novice ethnographer can collect all the necessary data using these tools. Some ethnographers also include their laptops in this kit, though this is a personal choice that has implications, which I discuss below. Many ethnographers use digital cameras to capture still photos. The problem with digital cameras is that, if anything, they're too easy to use. Novice ethnographers tend to snap away *ad infinitum*, resulting in far too many photos to sort through. I'll discuss more guidelines on how to use still photos in my section on conducting fieldwork. Suffice it to say here that digital cameras are a must-have, but remember the more data you collect, the more you have to analyze!

The Livescribe recording pen is a tool uniquely suited to the private-sector ethnographer. Unlike academic ethnographers, private-sector ethnographers rarely have the time or budget to transcribe interviews in their entirety. They instead must zero in on participants' key concerns quickly, which makes full transcription not only too labor-intensive but also not very useful. Instead, what private-sector ethnographers need is the ability to pluck out quotes quickly. This is precisely what the Livescribe pen allows them to do with audio recordings. The pen is an analogue pen with ink, but also a digital recorder. It comes with a special notebook that syncs the pen's interactions with the page with the audio recording. So if a participant says, "I find this registration process very confusing," the ethnographer can "favorite" that moment by clicking the "star" button in

Should You Use a Laptop in the Field?

Some ethnographers have practiced only with the aid of a laptop for note taking. The laptop has the advantage of the keyboard, which enables fast, verbatim note taking. However, it's unlikely that an ethnographer working alone can interview, observe, and take notes using a laptop, so a research assistant is usually required for a laptop to work well. One unique way to use the laptop is to use the audio recording functionality in Microsoft OneNote, while simultaneously taking typewritten notes. This syncs the audio recording to the notes, just like with the handwritten Livescribe notes. Using a laptop should not be done without consideration for rapport, however. Health research has shown that computer use can lessen rapport, so laptops should be used with care. Computer use in the physician's exam room, for example, has been shown to reduce rapport (Gadd and Penrod, 2000), but some of these effects can be mitigated by carefully placing a laptop so that it does not create a physical barrier between physician and patient (Ludwick and Doucette, 2009). Ethnographers who are comfortable taking notes on a laptop should consider that same careful placement and ensure that they make eye-contact with participants, which has been shown to cement social bonds in interactions involving high-technology use (Nardi and Whittaker, 2002).

the Livescribe notebook. Or perhaps the ethnographer can write a note like, "This is where registration breaks down." Later, when he is reviewing the recording, he can tap that note on his page, and the Livescribe pen will reproduce that exact moment in the audio recording. This revolutionized my practice! I now rarely worry about transcribing the entire interview. Instead, I focus on the key quotes or topics I've noted during the interview, and can easily transcribe these quotes in their entirety.

The smartphone can do several things while in the field. First, it allows you to keep track of where your participants are and how to get there. It is extremely useful in navigating unfamiliar terrain, and being able to call ahead if you are running late. Second, it doubles as a digital camera, if need be. I tend to use my Evernote app to capture images and tag them on as soon as I can. Third, your smartphone is a backup recorder for your Livescribe pen, should you have one. It also has the wonderful ability to turn you into a radio documentarian.

Ethnographers infrequently use audio as part of their final reports, which is a missed opportunity. In my former life as a journalist, I trained with some of the best radio documentary makers the Canadian Broadcasting Corporation ever produced. I learned from CBC Radio that audio can produce rich and illuminating stories, particularly when you hear participants' voices or the sounds of their environments. Just like there is "good television" in visually compelling results, there is "good radio" in compelling sounds. I recently used the audio of moving boxes around, recorded in my participants' homes, to demonstrate the inconvenience of pulling out the client's product when it was needed. Smartphones allow you to produce wonderful audio, either with the built-in audio recorder or with apps like Hindenburg Journalist, which is designed for journalists. Hindenburg allows you to simply tap your phone when a participant says or does something of interest. I use this tool alongside the Hindenburg desktop editing system, which allows you to mix up to three tracks into a single audio file. My past training in radio certainly helped me here, because editing audio takes as much time as editing video. But the richness the audio produces is wonderfully unexpected.

Many private-sector ethnographers consider video a must-have for research. I disagree. Like all these tools, video recorders do not compensate for poor ethnographic practice. Many novice ethnographers think that using video will ensure that they definitely capture important moments with participants. But all too often, what ends up happening is that instead of relying on ethnographic skill, the ethnographer simply captures countless hours of video that take untold days to analyze. Moreover, oftentimes novice ethnographers spend more time fiddling with their video equipment than actually interviewing their participants. Some of the best moments are lost because the video equipment gets more attention than their participants.

For this reason, I recommend using video equipment only if you are already familiar enough with video shooting. I myself am not confident in my ability to shoot video, so I either do not offer video as an output, or I hire a videographer to do that work specifically, freeing me up to do what I do best: interview and observe participants. If your project requires video, there are a few critical tools. A tripod (even a small one) will ensure that your video will not be jerky. Invest in a decent microphone so that your participants' voices will emerge clearly. A decent video camera is necessary, but you do not always need broadcast quality. Of course, you will also need video editing software. My friend and colleague Bruno Moynié, an ethnographic filmmaker, swears that Final Cut Pro is the only tool for this job, and I'm inclined to agree. For more insight on how to make resonant outputs other than video, please see Chapter 10, "Reporting."

Analysis Tools: Sifting Through

In this phase, your job is to reduce, synthesize, and visualize your data (Miles and Huberman, 1994). Ethnographers need to hierarchically organize data, visualize data, and synthesize data. Sadly, there are still too few tools that do this really well. If you've already used a digital capturing tool like Evernote during your fieldwork, you can actually use it to help you review and tag your notes. Unfortunately, Evernote still does not allow you to hierarchically organize your notes, nor does it allow you to visualize your information in any meaningful way.

Currently, the de facto tool for qualitative researchers is still NVivo. NVivo is the standard for academic ethnographers because it allows you to tag or "code" individual lines from interview transcripts. The quote is the "currency" that academic ethnographers use, so this is a must-have feature for them. But sadly, Nvivo has a terribly steep learning curve, a confusing mental model, and an incomprehensible nomenclature. Novice users must invest 10s if not 100s of hours figuring out the software before they can get value from it, and for private-sector ethnographers, the return on that investment is rather low. For that reason, I only recommend NVivo if your project is very long, which means you need excellent data management, or it is an academic project, which requires very deep analysis. There are similar software packages, such as Atlas.ti, MaxQDA, and QDA Miner, which are also designed for large-scale academic qualitative research projects. The private-sector ethnographer may find value in any one of these packages if he is interested in documenting his fieldnotes for the long term and in engaging in deep reading and analysis of interview transcripts.

Thankfully, there are new cloud-based tools that offer the important functions—hierarchical ordering, visualization, and data reduction—in a very light, web-based interface. A relatively new tool called Dedoose offers all that a private-sector ethnographer might need. It is still in its early release stages, so its functionality may be limited or lack fidelity, but it's a promising replacement for the "heavier" desktop software packages. Cloud-based tools have the added advantage of being easily updated by their makers, however. It's likely that Dedoose, for example, will expand its software functionality and device-specific tools (such as iPhone apps).. Tablet and smartphone-based data collection tools are likely to be added to these traditional tools, in time. Traditional, desktop-only tools like NVivo will become rapidly obsolete if they do not offer a cloud-based tool and multi-device collection services soon. The novice ethnographer would be well advised to start with a cloud-based tool, not a traditional desktop client, if they want their tool to remain up-to-date.

Reporting Tools: Telling Stories

When you report your ethnographic findings, you are not simply providing a summary of research findings. Instead, you are telling your participants' stories. You must do this in a format and manner that will make sense to your clients and stakeholders. Unfortunately, this almost always means creating a PowerPoint presentation (Keynote for Mac is a similar program). I will examine the nature of reporting ethnographic findings more thoroughly in Chapter 10, "Reporting," but for now, be aware that PowerPoint is only one of many software tools you can use to tell ethnographic stories. If you must use these software tools, at the very least consider how you might break the typical template. Consider starting with blank slides only, and then adding photos or text boxes from there. Most ethnographers would balk at creating solely a PowerPoint presentation as a report; I am one of those ethnographers! Consider also creating a document in a word processor like Microsoft Word or in a layout program like Adobe Illustrator (this is not for the faint of heart; only do this if you are a master in Illustrator).

Academically trained ethnographers tend to focus on the text more than the imagery, in part because this is what tools like Word afford. But visualizing data, particularly photographs, is a key aspect to communicating private-sector ethnographic findings. Ethnographers should look for tools that allow for the synthesis of disparate pieces of data. Photo slideshow or collage software and text visualization tools help here.

For text, consider experimenting with visualization tools such as Wordle, which allows you to create a "word cloud" of emergent themes. For images, I recommend using one of the many image collage applications. I use one called Shape Collage, which allows you to create a collage of digital images in various sizes and orientations. Shape Collage solves one of the biggest reporting problems: having to reduce down the number of photographs without reducing the nuance or insight these photos convey. TurboCollage also allows for the same functionality. I tend to use these tools for report cover sheets or introduction slides, but I also use them as a way of comparing the differences in participants' contexts.

If you have decided to use audio in your report, there are various audio slideshow tools that will help you put audio underneath a slideshow. This functionality is increasingly being bundled into operating systems like Mac OS and Windows 8, but these built-in tools are generally intended for "consumer" scenarios, such as making birthday or anniversary slideshows. The right tool for ethnographers is what software makers call a "point solution," or one that is intended specifically to time pictures to slide transitions, with a voice narrative. Apple's iPhoto allows you to do this with music, and quite easily. Microsoft's Movie Maker allows you to do this with a little more fidelity and control. I like to use SoundSlides Plus, which allows you to create an audio track (something I might have mixed separately in Hindenburg's audio desktop software), and then sync transitions precisely to changes in participant voices or contexts. Audio slideshow tools are only going to get simpler and more ubiquitous.

Once you've finished your ethnographic project, you will then have all of the data and reports to file. Start the cycle again. File your data in password protected tools like Evernote or your own computer's files structure.[4] Delete the files you will never need again. Back up your hard drive and make sure your computer is password protected. When it's time to start the next project, or better, just before it's time to start the next project, review your "files." Re-read your reports. Watch your finished videos. Re-read your original field notes. Consider what they mean. Make new connections to a colleague's report you just read.

Use of these tools will not automatically improve your ethnographic practice. Avoid the rookie mistakes of poorly stored data, morasses of unneeded photographs, or endless hours of mundane video footage. Resist the cheap trick of a flashy but superficial PowerPoint presentation. Like Mike Holmes, I encourage you to use these tools because they are the best that contemporary practice provides. But unlike Mike Holmes, I urge you to consider your own priorities. Does your design team really need a collage of images? Does your client really want an audio slide-show? Do you really have time to shoot and edit an entire video? Ask yourself which tools suit your particular purpose and, with practice, you will slowly transform from novice to master. By the time you have achieved ethnographic mastery, your tools will probably have evolved into an entirely new and unexpected set of devices and software.

Chapter 5
Managing Clients

When I first started ethnographic research back in the late '90s, there was someone who held a stake in my research. Remember my terrifyingly intelligent methods professor, Catherine? She was the first ethnographic mentor I had. For her class, I conducted a pilot study for what would eventually become my master's thesis. I consulted Catherine before I went into the field, showing her my interview guide and my general plan. She approved my approach and off I went. I had no idea what I was doing.

Sure enough, upon my return from my first ethnographic observation at a financial news web site, Catherine found my research to be less than it should be. I shouldn't have been surprised, given how little experience I had and how high her expectations were. My biggest surprise was that she actually *praised* what I considered to be mere journalistic flourishes. I had intentionally limited observational details in my initial report because I believed "academic" writing frowned upon such narrative tools. When Catherine gave me feedback on my pilot study, the most positive comment she gave was "Love it!" scribbled into the margin of what I considered rough observational notes. This was not at all what I had expected.

I learned then—and re-learned many times over—that clarity of expectations is incredibly important. Understanding what you're doing in the field is one thing; understanding what your client thinks you're

Practical Ethnography: A Guide to Doing Ethnography in the Private Sector by Sam Ladner, 69–86. © 2014 Left Coast Press, Inc. All rights reserved.

doing is a completely different thing. By "client," I mean the person you are helping improve a product or service. The "client" can be a product manager, a designer, a software engineer, or an executive. Ethnographers help these people improve what they are doing, so it's critical that they understand what the ethnographic research agenda involves. Private-sector ethnographers often bring their clients along with them into the field. It's very important that you ensure that they understand what ethnography is and what it will achieve.

Academic ethnographers do not have clients. To be sure they have funders, colleagues, research assistants, journal reviewers and editors, and all of these stakeholders affect how they design, conduct, and report their findings. But they do not have clients. Clients are a different type of stakeholder, with entirely different effects on ethnographic practice. This chapter is one that remains altogether missing from traditional methods text books; it is where I discuss the ways in which the client relationship affects ethnographic practice and how private-sector ethnographers can manage that process ethically, professionally, and successfully.

Rare is it when an internal ethnographer is directly responsible for designing a product or service, or crafting a marketing strategy herself. All private-sector ethnographers have clients in the sense that there are people who have a direct stake in the research project's outcome. Like funders and colleagues, clients have expectations. When they hire an external vendor, or task an internal ethnographer, they have pictures in their minds of what they will get when the research is complete. All too often, that picture differs from what they actually do get, which directly undermines the impact of the ethnographic project itself.

Sadly, private-sector ethnographers have few resources to draw upon to help them conceptualize the client relationship. Ethnography is by its very orientation a reflective practice, so, unsurprisingly, academic ethnographers have meditated extensively on the implications of having their various stakeholders in the outcome of ethnography. These kinds of analyses typically focus on participants' stake in the research. For example, Fine (1993) argues that there is an "underside" to ethnographic practice that often remains hidden from participants and even from ethnographers. He reviews the moral dilemmas ethnographers grapple with and asks questions such as, are we, in fact, the "friendly ethnographer," or is this a self we intentionally project to participants in order to get what we want? McCorkel and Myers (2003) point out that ethnographers usually occupy a position of privilege relative to their participants and, as such, must acknowledge and reflect upon what this implies for our practice. It is common for academic ethnographers to be in a position of superior power relative to their participants.

Ethnographers can also find themselves in a position of *inferior power*, relative to their participants, particularly when they are studying organizations at the behest of senior leaders. This is a common situation for organizational ethnographers, who are often caught within a web of hierarchies, even when they are academics with jobs at universities (Ybema, Yanow, Wels, and Kamsteeg, 2009). Whether occupying a position of greater or lesser power in relation to participants, ethnographers cannot escape their position vis-à-vis clients. Clients pay the bill. Clients can end a project. Clients can even end a career. This position is supremely precarious for the private-sector ethnographer in a way that the position of an academic ethnographer can never be. Private-sector ethnographers, however, are professionals, just like their academic counterparts. Just because a client ends a project does not mean the ethnographer ceases to be an ethnographer. It is this professional identity that can mitigate the precarity of the client-ethnographer relationship.

How can we manage this relationship? Private-sector ethnographers must ask slightly different questions than academic ethnographers because they manage client relationships. What is the nature of the ethnographic project within a corporate context? What does the corporate context imply for ethnographic practice? Private-sector practitioners themselves have offered some insight into the nature of this kind of ethnographic project, and the implications specific to the private sector. Mariampolski and Schlossberg (2007), for example, point out that good private-sector ethnography offers specific recommendations relating to the entire customer experience, and not just pieces of it. This differs from academic ethnography, which is typically focused on interpreting and theorizing about the implications of the cultural practices the ethnographer witnesses.

In their case study, Mariampolski and Schlossberg detail how a shopping checkout experience was improved by their observations of the customer purchasing journey from start to finish. Their recommendations focused on specific fixes to individual steps in the checkout process. This laser focus on making suggestions for improvement allows the ethnographer to maintain his professional identity as outside expert, hired specifically to observe, interpret, and critique the current situation. Unlike the academic ethnographer, the private-sector ethnographer must constantly consider what can be improved in the current state of affairs, and specifically how to improve it.

Designers and design researchers have also explored how to offer insight through ethnography, while maintaining a client relationship. Reese (2004), for example, conducted an ethnography of emergency medical technicians for a medical devices manufacturer. The device manufacturer had little insight into how EMTs actually used their tools, and Reese was able to uncover important unknown information for the client. Reese notes that deep insight into EMT culture helped the manufacturer design new devices that suited the EMTs' need for rapid "ramp up" to sudden crises. This marked a significant departure in how some people in the client organization perceived their roles. The key moment for change came when one member of the client's marketing team transformed his thinking from believing that his job was simply to convince customers to buy his products, to believing his task was to *create products customers actually want*. But while clearly this is a huge success of the empathetic standpoint of ethnography, Reese does not explain how this transformation comes to be or describe some of the pitfalls he faced along the way. How did he manage to convince the client to come along? What were the factors that led to his client's epiphany? It's not clear.

Some academics go as far as to condemn the outputs of private-sector ethnography altogether, arguing that ethnographic research is fundamentally at odds with the profit motive. Caron and Caronia (2007), for example, warn in their ethnography of teenagers' use of mobile phones that "advertising agencies" are using ethnography to better sell consumer goods to people. Implicit in their discussion is the condemnation of for-profit work, though they do not directly say so. One academic does directly grapple with this question. In his post for the wonderful sociology blog *Cyborgology*, David Banks[1] recently questioned the role of social scientists in business and, more specifically, in the technology sector.

He asked whether it was possible for questions of inequality to be asked. For example, is it possible to design an anti-racist Reddit.com? But more importantly, Banks questioned whether social scientists would ask those questions in the context of business to begin with. This is indeed the fundamental question about private-sector ethnography. Can we use the emic position, when our clients' stated profit motive often leads to an etic position? And if so, how do we go about doing this in a productive way?

What Is "Private-Sector Ethnography"?

In their wonderful book, *Doing Anthropology in Consumer Research*, Patricia Sunderland and Rita Denny (2007) offer a very simple rubric for understanding the symbolic nature of any social phenomenon. As I mentioned in Chapter 2, they suggest that we ask simply: What is "blank"? They use the example of coffee, noting that it is indeed a hot, brown liquid but it is also a way to bond over business, or to create a new social relationship in a low-intimacy fashion.

What is a "private-sector ethnographic project"? On the surface, it is a research project designed to uncover contextual insights for use in design and marketing. But, as I discussed also in Chapter 2, ethnography is essentially an epistemological shift, forcing its practitioners to empathize with participants and adopt their standpoint. Taken in this way, then, private-sector ethnography (when done correctly) is essentially what Alvesson and Sveningson call "culture change work" (2008). In their study of a technology spin-off company, Alvesson and Sveningsson argue that the very act of asking questions about cultural practice is changing how a culture works; self-reflexivity is not a practice that most organizations prize or engage in. Asking what consumers truly believe about a company's product is a bold act because it begs a self-examination of *what the company believes* about that same product.

Culture change work is the process by which organizations change norms, values, and behaviors. We often conceive of organizational culture change as a linear "project," and not the culmination of shifts in a multitude of many micro-processes. Culture change work is not something that is "directed" by senior management, although it may start there. It is embodied by everyday practices by all members of the organization. A private-sector ethnography project is a micro-process that shifts individual actors' norms, values, and behaviors. Ethnographic practice is fundamentally reflexive and emic in its standpoint, which may represent a significant departure from existing norms, values, and behaviors in contemporary organizations. Through their participation in your ethnography, your clients are slowly beginning to embrace the emic perspective, which can be a significant change in how they have understood their work until that point. This is why private-sector ethnography is so powerful, but it is also why it is often met with outright resistance from client organizations.

The corporate world is riddled with the corpses of failed culture change projects. The true embrace of the customer's perspective faces steep hurdles in most organizations, due to the nature of organizations themselves. It seems logical that everyone who works at a mobile phone company would want to design and sell better mobile phones. Yet, an ethnographic study detailing how their phone is not working well for customers may be a threatening finding. The woes of Canadian smartphone maker, BlackBerry, are a case in point. The company has a well-established research discipline, with full-time researchers. Yet with all this research, the declining popularity of the flagship product came as a great surprise to the co-CEOs, who were eventually forced to resign .

Organizations are self-sustaining machines. They have a remarkable capacity to stave off threatening states in order to perpetuate themselves. Anyone who has worked in an organization facing stiff competition will have seen this first hand—any mention of the competitor's superiority will be met with downward glances, the quiet shuffling of feet, or even a chorus of outright disagreement. Ethnographic projects represent a fundamental threat to identity if they focus on the gap between the customer's experience and the organization's own identity pillars. It is almost a "stress response," wherein the organization attacks ideas that are seen as a threat to its "body." As Tuckman and Jensen (1977) famously described, groups form, then "storm," before finally setting "norms," at which point they spend time agreeing, over and over. Organizations aspire to continue to agree. Woe is the hapless ethnographer that introduces an entirely new "storm" to an established organization.

Ethnography as Pandora's Box

Ethnography is still a rather unusual type of research project for most private-sector organizations. There are some organizations that have deep familiarity with ethnography, such as Xerox PARC, for example. Brigitte Jordan's pioneering ethnographic research at Xerox now has deep roots in the organization, making it possible for ethnographers there to rely on organizational history to smooth the way for ethnographic practice. But for a typical private-sector ethnographer, his clients will be relatively unfamiliar with the nature of the work and how it differs fundamentally from other kinds of market research, such as focus groups and surveys. This lack of familiarity often means that clients are deeply surprised by the kinds of findings ethnography typically offer. They may be expecting a list of "themes," as from a focus group, or a chart summarizing "the numbers," as with a survey. Instead, they may receive a holistic and detailed analysis of how their entire customer journey is broken, or perhaps a carefully articulated metaphor that summarizes their customers' belief systems. This is surprising, to say the least. It can also, in the best cases, be the seed for culture change work.

Design professor Peter Jones described a form of culture change in his detailed case study of an interaction design project. In his tellingly titled monograph, "We Tried To Warn You," (2008) he notes that the design process itself transformed his clients' thinking about their customers and how they relate to them. He notes that the moment of truth came when his clients viewed critically their own positions and how they related to their customers. His frank description of the dicey moments of client resistance to this critical reflection conveys the treacherous nature of ethnographic research in the private sector; clients themselves may have no idea what a project may open up for them.

In her paper on using ethnography at Microsoft, Donna Flynn (2009) offers some insight into how such processes play out in everyday corporate life. She notes that in her experience, when she offered research findings about customers, program managers tended to discount her findings, saying that "my customers are different." She argues that this act of resistance is a way to create distance between the eth-nographer and the customer, and for the program manager to assert "superior" knowledge of the customer. The ethnographer is not the expert, the program manager is. This process is one of many such gam-bits that members of client organizations will play in order to maintain order and perpetuate the status quo within the organization. It is an almost automatic response to disruption. The private-sector ethnogra-pher should expect it and not take it personally.

Key Client Management Tasks

The key client-management task, then, is for the ethnographer both to educate his clients on the craft of ethnography and to prepare them for the potentially disruptive aspects of ethnographic research. To achieve this, he must take on the role of empathetic educator. He must be clear about how ethnography strives to take the participant's perspective in his work. Even though he may never be truly successful in that endeavor, his clients should know that this is his stated goal. He must also be clear about what kinds of data and reports he will produce. Clients may be accus-tomed to reviewing preliminary quantitative data while the researcher is in the field. The ethnographer must set the expectations with clients on how much, if any, preliminary insight he will be able to offer during the research phase. Ethnographic research is often very messy in that it changes. Ethnographers often must simply respond to the participants' desires, which may mean changing the interview guide on the fly, or accommodating their wish for privacy of a certain location or topic. This is not at all unusual in ethnographic research, though clients may not understand this prior to their engagement with ethnography.

The second activity in client management is to be a culture change agent, as much as possible. For this task, the ethnographer must play a role similar to Simmel's (1950) famous "stranger"; the ethnographer is not a member of the organization and can therefore play an important role in change. She can represent the "other" and bring with her values, behaviors, and beliefs that may differ from the organization's. Because she is an outsider, she is a neutral and safe confidante for members to share intimate details that may be counter to the organization's stated goals. Clients can speak to the ethnographer honestly about their own product's shortcomings because, unlike their colleagues, she holds no stake in the perpetuation of the organization. A brand manager can tell her honestly that the product is confusing to customers. An interaction designer can confide that he has never been able to sketch out the product's mental model. The ethnographer can also bring with her ideas and practices that may be new or unusual, and because she is not a member of the organization, these kinds of practices may be permitted. Organization members may also be permitted to engage in such practices so long as she is there. In short, her role is to be the professional outsider, with the express and clear purpose of effecting change within the organization. This culture change work is not for the faint of heart, and at times feels entirely ineffective. But it behooves private-sector ethnographers to know that this unstated activity is at the root of ethnography's transformative power. Strangers have played a significant role in changing society, as Simmel details about the role European Jews played in commerce. It is entirely possible for private-sector ethnographers to play a similar role within their client organizations.

Being a "stranger" is difficult for internal ethnographers, but as Flynn suggests, it is not impossible. It requires an even keel, and a keen practice of reflexivity. As an external ethnographer, it is easy to have clients confide in you. But as an internal ethnographer, your clients may very well be those with whom you work most closely. This makes it extremely difficult for stakeholders to be honest, and it also means that the ethnographer herself has a stake in the perpetuation of the organization. The ethnographer may find herself wanting to defend the product, or to discount criticism. Defeating this requires an entirely different set of skills—namely, the ability to cultivate a healthy disinterest in the outcome of the research, and also the ability to couch negative findings in positive ways.

Ethnographer as Educator

How should ethnographers educate and prepare their clients for their own ethnographic journey? The most important education is that of ethnography's inherent critical epistemology. The participant's standpoint is incredibly difficult to embrace for many organizations because it is often considered diametrically opposed to business success. As Raphael

Designers as Clients

Design ethnography is specifically targeted to either creating or improving a product or service. Designers need specific recommendations for how to design their product or service, and may resist long reports that seem more like useless stories about characters. They need direction on what to build. Designers in particular need for ethnographic insights to be dynamic and experiential in nature. R. J. Anderson (1994) argues that designers gravitate to ethnography when they become disenchanted with traditional "requirements gathering" research methods, which are more suited to engineering than to empathetic design. But designers are often unfamiliar with ethnography as a method. Designers, according to Anderson, see ethnography primarily as a form of data collection, not as a way of looking at the world or as an epistemological position. By this he means that designers do not typically understand that the ethnographer's eye is always interpretive, and not an unbiased, passive collection of observable events. Standing in a room and looking at things is not ethnography. He argues that designers' need to understand what consumers' lives are like often does not require ethnography at all. To get a feel for what consumers want and need, designers may not need ethnography at all. In fact, according to Anderson, designers are profoundly disappointed when they discover ethnography is, at its heart, an analytic lens, and not a data capturing method. He argues that "brokenness is in the eye of the beholder." By this, he means that designers often use their own standpoint in deciding what is actually broken. Designers may mistake noticing "what's broken" for what a consumer wants or needs, when really what matters is what the consumer wants. If a consumer does not think a sign-up process is frustrating, it is not broken. If a consumer does not see usability problems with software, it is not broken. If a consumer does not find anything wrong with his existing teapot, it is not broken. Designers must first learn to adopt the consumers' standpoint, and appreciate his needs from their perspective. This is the primary way in which designers can benefit from ethnography, and it is the primary challenge for ethnographers to show designers what a consumer's standpoint really is.

Ramirez and Jerome Ravetz (2011) note, this organizational response is related to organizational identity—findings that somehow threaten the core of a company's identity are likely to be perceived as threatening and therefore not true. This is particularly relevant for ethnographic findings.

Table 3: Typical Client Management Problems and Suggested Solutions

Problem	Source	Potential Solution
Resistance to going into the field	Lack of familiarity or discomfort with meeting actual customers	Pre-fieldwork training session with role playing and how-to
Disbelief of findings	Positivist orientation; lack of familiarity with qualitative validity	Comprehensive list of all data points collected (see Table 4, Data Points Collected in a Recent Workplace Ethnography, for an example)
Discomfort with "negative" findings	Threat to organizational or even personal identity	Framing findings as perceptions people hold, not the "truth"

Often, ethnographers will find deep empathy with their participants' experiences with a company's product or service. These very real consumer experiences are often not what company employees consider to be "true," and to have these real, raw, and sometimes unpleasant experiences laid bare is to threaten organizational identity directly. For this reason, ethnographers must prepare ahead of time for this organizational response. This means setting the stage for these kinds of findings before ever going into the field. Your clients should know that they may hear things they will dislike or that they will disagree with.

Taking clients along on fieldwork is a transformative experience. As philosopher Hubert Dreyfus (2009) tells us, there is nothing more effective for learning new things than the physical discomfort of being out of your element. Dreyfus is referring to the irreplaceability of face-to-face learning, but the underlying principle is the same: clients are often deeply affected by fieldwork. Many of them have never met a real customer, and certainly not in that customer's own home or office. The client will see, touch, and smell the real world of their customer. They may learn why their product seems irrelevant to that customer, or why their service provides nothing but frustration. If it is possible to have a client come with you to at least one field visit, do it.

Educate your clients before you go into the field. Hold a meeting or presentation to explain what ethnography is, and why it differs. Give real examples of discomfort or threatening findings that you or other ethnographers have uncovered in the past. Equip your clients with that knowledge, and they will not be surprised when the findings come back.

Perhaps the most important way to educate clients is to take them into the field with you. Without exception, every client I have taken into the field with me has experienced a degree of transformation that simply does not happen with other types of research methods. I had one client complain to me about the participants in a recent focus group she observed. She was researching young women's beliefs about their own sexual health. As she sat behind the glass, she said she found herself increasingly angry at the participants inside. The participants were all about 20 years old and seemed concertedly unconcerned about this topic. She found their responses flippant, uninformed, and rather irresponsible. Her anger only grew as the focus group continued. Her genuine concern for the young women's health had morphed into anger. Now imagine if the research had been ethnography instead of a focus group.

Preparing Clients for the Field Visit

What to Expect on Ethnographic Interviews
The following is a brief explanation of what an ethnographic interview entails. It is intended to provide non-researchers with a set of expectations so that they will get the most out of the experience.

How Ethnographic Interviews Differ
First, ethnographic interviews often do not follow a set pattern. The interview should flow naturally, so the researcher may choose to ask some questions before others, if the situation requires it. The process may feel circuitous at times, but eventually all research themes will be covered. Secondly, ethnographic interviews also involve observation. The researcher will take you to the site of interest [a home, an office, or even a car] and may ask the participant to show or describe particular objects.

The Interview: A Description
The ethnographic interview begins when the researcher and you arrive at the site. Together, you will knock on the door and be greeted by the participant.

Ethnographic observation begins right away, as the researcher will be noting objects of interest. The researcher will begin by asking the participant to show the area or site of interest. Conversation will arise naturally at this point. This could last to estimate: consider what tasks you need the participant to perform. After visiting or touring the site the group will sit down for a discussion, usually lasting about an hour. This is the heart of the interview, which will be followed by the participant showing the researcher the topic, product, or service of interest.

Your Role

People who accompany the researcher are introduced as a "note taker," and their company name is not revealed until the end of the interview. The company's name is not a secret, but it is better if participants feel they can be honest about how they feel. As note taker, your job is primarily to take notes and notice objects and symbols in the home. Listen to the conversation and jot down anything that you find interesting.

At the beginning of the interview, you may feel that the researcher is not getting to the point or asking the right questions. There is a reason for this: the first priority is to create rapport, which essentially boils down to trust. A good interview is like a dance—with the interviewee leading. The researcher is deeply experienced in the semi-structured interview technique and will cover all relevant topics.

Feel free to ask a question, if you have one. But be aware that the researcher is strategically guiding the conversation.

Following the interview, set aside 20 minutes to write down your impressions. Try to do this as soon after the interview as possible; you will remember far more. Write a brief summary of the discussion. Synthesize or clarify the notes you took during the interview. Try to come up with five or six major themes that you noticed.

Tips to Remember:
1. Arrive five minutes early to meet the researcher.
2. Smaller, hard-sided notebooks (not 8 ½" by 11") are easier to take notes with. Avoid company branded notebooks!
3. Bring an extra pen, just in case.
4. Review the interview guide.
5. Dress as if you were attending a casual coffee date with a work colleague.
6. Go with the flow.

She would have visited a young woman in her home, perhaps. She would have spent time talking with her, sitting next to her, and seeing the intimate atmosphere of her kitchen or even her bedroom. In those few moments she spent attending to this participant's home and life, she would have learned more about her, perhaps even being transported into the time when she too was young and naïve. She would have learned more about the day-to-day struggles of creating an adult identity in today's world, simply by being with this young woman in her own context. Even if that young woman had been as flippant and uninformed as the focus group attendees, the client would have already been better equipped to empathize with this young woman's life, just by being with her in an intimate setting.

If you do choose to take clients with you, I recommend that you hold a preparatory meeting, in which you discuss your expectations of them and what they can expect from the field visit.

Ethnographer as Culture Change Agent

As a change agent, the ethnographer must consider herself first and foremost an outsider. Her role is to bring new ideas or techniques to the client organization and to act as "stranger confidante" to client stakeholders. She must organize her ideas and recommendations in relation to common practice within the organization. This means understanding the organization's dominant method of "truth," which could be science-based, or perhaps more rooted in the words of the organization's leaders. She should be aware of when her ideas and recommendations conflict with dominant practice, and devise ways to point out the gap in a nonthreatening way.

The ethnographer as culture change agent is a difficult role, to say the least. You are often thwarted in your efforts. You are often told you are an outsider. But over time, with good relationships, you can effect incremental change in tiny nuggets and slivers of hope. This is especially true for internal ethnographers who work on multiple projects, over time, with an array of individuals within their organization. But it can also be true for ethnographers outside client organizations. You may not effect significant organizational change in the first project, and maybe not even the second, but with every field visit, every surprising finding, you will plant seeds of change within individuals' minds, perhaps without even realizing it. Internal ethnographers must have even more fortitude. They must occupy an insider's position and at the same time rock the boat with uncomfortable knowledge. Doing this takes more than a little courage, and a very deft hand.

Once ethnographers return from the field, there is another opportunity to help clients embrace change. Face-to-face meetings provide a moment of potential culture change, if ethnographers use this "deft hand" well. One ethnographer who studied Portuguese wine found himself in the middle of an awkward situation. Pedro Oliveira had been hired by a wine company he calls "Old Portugal" to investigate how the company should innovate on their branding and marketing messages. Oliveira engaged in what he called "peer dinners," in which the ethnographer shares a meal with consumers, while observing wine drinking behavior at the same time (Oliveira, 2012). His research found that consumers perceived his client's product to be more about sharing time with family than it was about objectively good wine attributes such as taste and bouquet. Understandably, the client bristled at this finding.

Oliveira describes the moment as an awkward pause in a face-to-face workshop. His clients focused on a single PowerPoint slide on the screen, which suggested that their product was not objectively as good as their competitors products. He and his agency colleagues shifted tactics, and invited the client to consider the "brand" as something people construct. People includes the employees of the wine company, but also their friends and families, as well as "average consumers." From this view, the "bad" research findings are not about the product, but about how people perceive the product. This "deft hand" shows how the clients needed a safe way to explore how and why their product was not performing as well as other products. But they needed to grasp onto something that made their product—and therefore themselves—still "good."

Market researchers sometimes present consumers' perceptions of a product's attributes such as quality, design, or usability as "failures" if the product doesn't measure up to its competitors. It's no wonder that clients reject such findings, even if they are absolutely true. Instead of presenting consumers' perceptions as "failures," ethnographers can present these findings as "beliefs." Isn't it amazing that there is such a wide gap between the clients' beliefs and the consumers' beliefs? Why would that be? What kinds of activities are we as a company engaging in that would facilitate such consumer perceptions? It is this kind of conversation that opens a safe space for hard conversations. An invididual client may wish to acknowledge her failures in product support, for example, but can only do so if she affirms that the product and the company are still "good." The "deft hand," therefore, involves equal measures of affirmation and the interrogation of consumer perceptions.

After educating and facilitating culture change, the ethnographer will have planted the seeds for future transformation. The challenge at this point is to maintain the momentum of positive change that ethnography begins. Ethnographers who work within organizations find it difficult to maintain this momentum, while consulting ethnographers, who work outside the organization, must rely on their clients to maintain this positive change.

I wish I had known to ask my professor Catherine more about her expectations. I wish I had known what she assumed about my participants. I wish I had been better equipped to understand how hard organizational change really is. But over the years of practicing ethnography in the private sector, I have learned that culture is malleable. It has fissures ready to be cracked and loose threads ready to be pulled. Every organization can achieve some measure of change, however small. Every client can be nudged toward the emic position, however slowly. The ethnographer's role as educator and culture change agent is indeed a challenging one, but not an impossible one.

Techniques for Culture Change Agents

Culture change means shifting norms, values, beliefs, and assumptions within organizations. There are ways to manage this process.

1. Make alliances: Internal and external ethnographers should both focus on developing alliances with people who set norms and values—and they aren't always the most senior people. As any successful sales person will tell you, secretaries and administrators are some of the most important individuals in any organization because they set norms for seemingly mundane practices. If these practices symbolically communicate conservatism, the organization will have difficulty changing. Of course, those in senior roles also set the tone for what is acceptable and what is not. Ethnographers can focus on potential allies in these roles and support them as people who may potentially be frustrated with the lack of customer centricity in their organizations.

2. Construct symbols: Do not underestimate the power of the symbol for revealing potentially difficult ideas. The symbol can serve as a quickly understood but deeply meaningful concept that encapsulates complex ideas. In their study of architect Frank Gehry's firm, Yoo, Boland and Lyytinen (2006) noted that the firm had the opportunity to make a sculpture for the Barcelona Olympics in 1994. They used this opportunity to push the limits of their design and technical abilities. They created a "fish sculpture," which involved a very challenging 3D modeling process. From there on, the "fish sculpture" became a symbol of their willingness to try new things and to innovate existing processes. The symbol can also be the source of culture change.

   For example, in one project, I conducted an ethnography of two merging organizations. I realized my findings would reveal what anthropologist Elizabeth Coulson once called "uncomfortable knowledge" (as quoted in Ramírez and Ravetz, 2011, p. 480). But in my role as "stranger confidante," I had also learned that many in the client organization wanted this uncomfortable knowledge to be revealed. So in my recommendations, I suggested creating art installations that individuals throughout the organization could adapt or add to, and displaying the installations in prominent, high-traffic areas. The aim with this recommendation was to introduce the symbolic representation of uncomfortable truth, which is entirely less threatening than explicit discussions. The interactive nature of the installation was to invite individuals to symbolically embrace these ideas in a non-threatening way. Unfortunately, my recommendations were not taken up by the client organization. But on the other hand, dozens of people participated in that project, discussed the potential for change, and had genuinely honest moments with each other. This was a kernel of culture change that they all remember.

3. Build social capital: Sociologists often like to refer to social capital simply as "trust." Economists often measure social capital as a proxy for innovative capacity. Organizations that have difficulties changing often lack trust. In his book on social capital, Mario Luis Small (2009) examined the features of organizations that fostered social capital. He found that regular, frequent, and non-competitive contact between people was a great way to form bonds. For example, planning the annual Christmas party is a regular, non-competitive, and frequent opportunity to build trust between people. Ethnographers can encourage such interactions over time—especially internal ethnographers who may have a longer time horizon in which to effect change.

Chapter 6
Ethical Ethnography

When I worked as a journalist, my nod to ethical practice was to tell participants that I was recording the conversation. Occasionally, I forgot to do even that. So long as I did not misquote them, or broadcast their voices without their consent, I figured I still acted ethically. I had learned that, according to Canadian law, recording a conversation was legal as long as one party agreed to the recording (I always agreed). I never once asked an interviewee for informed consent in the shape of a release form. In fact, when I did my master's thesis, I interviewed journalists and accordingly asked them to sign an informed consent form approved by my university. Many of them laughed. "Are you serious?" one asked. Most commented they would never meet their deadlines if they had to have every interviewee sign a form. I agreed with them, and acknowledged it was a burden but it was how things were done in academia.

Oh, what I didn't know!

Ethical ethnographic practice is so much more than having participants "sign a form." It is not simply a stodgy academic ritual. Ethical practice is a way of conducting oneself. It is a value system, dare I say, even a culture that has been built over a century of practice (give or take a few decades). Private-sector ethnography is still creating its own culture; it is distinct from traditional academic ethnography, which has a more established method of practice. There is remarkably little discussion

Practical Ethnography: A Guide to Doing Ethnography in the Private Sector by Sam Ladner, 87–99. © 2014 Left Coast Press, Inc. All rights reserved.

about private-sector ethical practice, compared to the tomes of ethical debates produced in academia. Its standards of ethical practice are still relatively underdeveloped.

Yet, private-sector ethnography is not an entirely new phenomenon either. In their review of business anthropology, Allen Batteau and Carolyn Psenka (2012) argue that business anthropology dates back as many as 80 years, to the famous Hawthorne Experiments on workplace productivity. These studies were observational, but not purely "ethnographic" in that they did not focus on culture per se. These early forays into the workplace, followed by the pioneering work by researchers like Brigitte Jordan at Xerox PARC, have now blossomed into a full, rich community of researchers who work in advertising, market research, design, and technology, and gather yearly at the Ethnographic Praxis in Industry Conference (EPIC). Ethical debates emerge at EPIC and on AnthroDesign, a thriving listserv moderated by private-sector anthropologist Natalie Hanson. Yet even with this growing community, a robust framework for ethical practice of private-sector ethnography remains somewhat elusive. Some members of this community have attempted to fill this gap. Gerald Lombardi (2009), for example, has argued that the outsourcing of ethnographic interpretation or analysis to other ethnographers threatens our ability to treat each other ethically—and leads to the deskilling of ethnographic labor.

The major dilemma private-sector ethnography presents is the concept that business is inherently corrupt. I would argue that this conception is largely a symbolic division constructed by ethnographers to shore up the fiction that ethnography, however practiced, is never corrupt or exploitative. We humans create such divisions all the time. Anthropologist Mary Douglas (1972) traces the symbolic division between "clean" and "dirty" in her research on the "purity" of the home. Outside is "dirty," and dirt belongs outside the home. Likewise, sociologist Christena Nippert-Eng (1996) argues that the work/home divide is largely symbolic, and people use artifacts such as calendars and keys to mark this symbolic division. When one's "work" calendar is mixed with one's "personal" calendar, Nippert-Eng argues this is a symbolic welcoming of work into the home—a privilege enjoyed by those who have autonomy at work.

Batteau and Psenka (2012) exhort anthropologists to be "willing to work *inside* business, to get our hands dirty, and not simply observe the corporate world from a comfortable distance" (2012, p. 82, emphasis in original). They specifically refer to "dirty hands" several times in their review, implying that business anthropology is somehow considered "dirty." They go on to observe that an ethnographer can "return" from immersing herself in business. Return to where exactly? If one already works in business, to where is one returning? The implication here is that "inside" business is "dirty" and one "returns" to a clean place which is "outside" business. The ethnographer makes field trips into business to "get dirty," only to return to what the authors call the "comfortable distance" where one is "clean." This necessarily implies that there is a "pure" version of anthropology, one which is not inside business, but outside it. This clean/dirty framing reveals what some people implicitly assume about private-sector ethnography: that there is something inherently impure about business itself.

I reject this contention.

Ethnography has a dubious history of ethical conduct, even within the supposedly "pure" academic sector. In its earliest days, ethnography became a symbol of colonialism (and in some cases, its overt accomplice). In order to gain access to sites of study, anthropologists were frequently required to comply with colonialist conquerors' demands, which often included casting their participants as primitive savages, or peoples needing the civilizing influences of their colonial masters. Ethnographers who refused were denied further access to their sites and even blacklisted academically. Max Gluckman, for example, described his native South African participants as part of the heterogonous cultural fabric of the country, and not as "savages" as South Africa's apartheid rulers imagined them to be. He was publicly criticized for "going native" and even accused of being a Communist (Ader, 2011). Blacklisting and academic humiliation were real threats to ethnographers who questioned the "noble savage" paradigm. Many did not.

Contemporarily, academic ethical debates about ethnographic practice tend to focus on power differentials between participants and researchers. These debates can inform private-sector ethnographers about privilege, but they still do not address the clean/dirty divide. Jill McCorkel and Kristin Myers (2003), for example, analyze what rights their participants could really claim, given that they were inmates in prison. They explore the intersectionality of their privilege over these participants, which included both a class and a racial dimension. They adopt Dorothy Smith's "standpoint theory" to examine the role the institution (in this case, the prison) plays in these participants' lived experience, and they interrogate themselves and their motivations to produce research, given the necessarily coercive nature of the prison as an institution. Pertti Alasuutari argues that this power dynamic is unavoidable: "An encounter between two people who are beyond and outside all hierarchies and power relations is unthinkable; it is quite simply not a possibility" (1995, p.89). In their study of mobile phone use among teenagers, Andre Caron and Letizia Caronia (2007) note that mobile phone use is a way for teenagers to construct an identity, but one that often reinforces the stereotype that they are "lazy." It is this identity process they highlight, while at the same time, as "hard-working" adults, they held a position of power over the teenagers they studied, making it difficult to understand this self-conception without evoking their own position of power and privilege. University-based researchers have privilege, and ethnographic research brings that privilege into stark relief, particularly when the study focuses on some facet of inequality itself. This is often true for sociological studies of class, for example.

But none of these ethnographers discuss the very real challenge of negotiating a potentially corrupting position of doing research for profit. In the private sector, ethnographic practice faces all of these same problems of privilege, but there is a much deeper problem that must be confronted: private-sector ethnography's purpose is, at its heart, to generate more profit. Whether it be a marketing study on women's experiences of personal-care products, a design study of kitchens and stoves, or an organizational study of how employees use a new technology, private-sector ethnographers' ultimate goal is to sell more products, design better products that will sell more, or design a technology that enables an employer to extract more surplus value from its employees. An academic ethnographer may confront his own motivation to get grant money, to publish more for greater esteem, and ultimately for personal gain in the form of tenure. But a private-sector ethnographer must grapple with the fact that her research may lead to greater profits and, ultimately, the perpetuation of capitalism itself.

Is this an essentially unethical activity? Does generating more profit necessarily imply a breach of morals? Does participating in the capitalist system lead to a corruption of the emic ethnographic project? Melissa Cefkin flatly rejects this view in her book, *Ethnography and the Corporate Encounter*. Cefkin eschews "angst-ridden hand wringing about practitioners' moral and political complicity" (2009, p. 2). She argues that private-sector ethnography is about understanding what people produce, and in what ways. It is the legitimate study of market activity, which is one of the most basic forms of human expression. Why should we not study market activity from inside the market?

I would argue that studying market-based activity does not corrupt the emic position, at least not necessarily. If an academic ethnographer can act ethically while at the same time receiving the personal benefit of tenure, the private-sector ethnographer can conduct research that brings her clients greater profit without compromising the autonomy of her participants. It is a pleasant fiction to believe that one can achieve a "pure" ethnographic practice simply by studying from a "comfortable distance." A purist interpretation of capitalism construes any profit-seeking as necessarily "corrupting" a social interaction, but this overestimates the division between market activity and everyday life. There are frequent and common breaches of money transactions into even the most intimate relationships, yet this supposed corruption does not destroy these intimate relationships.

Sociologist Viviana Zelizer (2007) argues convincingly that it is a purist (and largely fictional) belief that social life can be extricated from the market. She suggests it is this belief that leads social actors to reconceptualize their money transactions as more "pure" social activities through sometimes elaborate explanations and workarounds. As a business owner, for example, I may pay my husband as a salaried employee, but I might recast his role as trusted advisor, not employee, in order to shore up the fiction that he is not financially dependent on and perhaps even exploited by me. Such workarounds allow us to believe that relationships are somehow outside the capitalist economy, and therefore uncorrupted. But in the end, my husband is both my employee and my husband; just because I pay him a salary does not necessarily corrupt our intimate relationship. Zelizer notes that such breaches happen regularly, yet neither the market nor intimate relations are fundamentally altered by them.

The division between the market and other social interactions may be largely symbolic. The market regularly and pervasively penetrates everyday life. The essential ethical dilemma for private-sector ethnographers is therefore not "How do I avoid the corrupting influence of market-based profits?" but rather, "How do I avoid the corrupting influence of personal gain?" In other words, the ethical dilemma is essentially the same as the "pure" academic practice. Just like academic ethnographers, private-sector ethnographers can find themselves confronted with a potential for personal (or corporate) gain at the expense of their participants. An academic ethnographer must confront her potential personal gain from extracting information from her participants in the form of publications, a salary, and tenure. A private-sector ethnographer must confront her potential gain from the same process, but this gain also includes a much more aggregate gain: that of her company selling more products, potentially at the expense of her participants and consumers in general. The academic ethnographer's gain is personal; the private-sector ethnographer's gain is more systemic and potentially reifying.

Ethical principles from traditional ethnography can still apply, therefore, to private-sector ethnography, with some adaptations to suit the unique challenges of working in industry. The American Anthropological Association (AAA) offers a starting point for the ethical principles we can apply. The AAA has distilled its ethical principles down to three simple statements:

1. Do no harm.
2. Be open and honest.
3. Gain informed consent.

These principles are generally applicable to private-sector ethnography as well, but with a few differences.

How Ethics Differ in Private-Sector Ethnography

The first major difference focuses on the notion of deceit. While ethnographers do engage in deceit in academia, in the private sector, deceit is usually related to a very specific problem: do you reveal your company or client name to participants? This is the essence of the private-sector ethnographer's grappling with "Be open and honest."

In academic ethnography, Sudhir Venkatesh (2008) caused a great deal of consternation when he conducted an ethnography of gang life in Chicago and was taken into the inner circle of a drug-dealing gang. It is hotly debated how transparent he was with his participants. This kind of ethical problem is what Fine (1993) refers to as a moral dilemma of the "ethnographic self." He argues that we grapple with a self-identity in the field, constructing one of three selves: the "chaste ethnographer," the "candid ethnographer," or the "fair ethnographer." Did Venkatesh act as the "chaste ethnographer" in his participant observation of gang life? This is perhaps one of the more extreme examples of the question of deceit in academic ethnography. But being the "chaste ethnographer" in the private sector is complicated by the hegemony of the "factist" perspective, which presupposes that honesty will necessarily corrupt the results.

In the private sector, being "open and honest" necessarily means confronting the problem of revealing the sponsoring company's name. Obscuring the company name in private-sector ethnography is not only relatively ineffective, it is corrosive and damaging. When forced to conceal the company's name, the ethnographer finds himself intentionally deceiving the participant specifically for the purpose of generating profit. In market research, this tradition of obscuring or actively concealing the company commissioning the research is based on the mistaken belief that participants' knowledge of the sponsor will bias the results. Most market researchers come from the psychological or factist tradition, which presupposes that a lack of bias is even possible. As I noted in Chapter 1, the interpretive method considers a lack of bias effectively impossible, so obscuring the company name adds little value to the quality of the findings. Worse, however, participants are left with no understanding of who might be learning about them, for what purpose, and to what end. This kind of deceit does nothing to improve the research outcomes and simply serves to corrode the relationship between ethnographer and participant.

In their recent paper, Eduardo Goncalves and Marcelo Fegundes (2013) tackled this very problem. Their client, a women's beauty products company, initially asked for the company's name to be hidden from the mostly rural Brazilian women the two ethnographers were studying. The client worried about bias and that participants would intentionally offer worse opinions of the company were they to know who the company was. But in the end, these researchers found that revealing the company's name had the opposite effect: once they knew the name of the company, participants were even more trusting and open.

Deceit is not necessary and actually causes harm. For these reasons, private-sector ethnographers should be very clear with their participants about the nature of their research, including the study sponsors. This is sometimes difficult to achieve because clients unfamiliar with ethnographic method will specifically ask that their company's name be anonymous, because they have the mistaken belief that "unbiased" insight can only come when the company's identity is hidden. I usually advise clients that we can begin the visit without disclosing the company name, eventually disclosing it during the interview itself, thereby offering an opportunity for participants to voice their opinions freely. Like Goncales and Fegundes, I have found that participants are curious about the sponsoring company and take delight in the moment of its reveal. It is also a moment of rapport building in the interview, wherein the participant feels as if she were an insider, taken into confidence. At this point, she is often willing to share an even more honest opinion because of this symbolically rich moment of reciprocal secrecy. The timing of this disclosure is tricky. I often wait until sufficient rapport is built with participants, either half-way through or at the end of the interview.

The second major difference between academic ethics and private-sector ethics involves informed consent. Informed consent requires some adaptation to the private sector. In academic ethnography, informed consent involves telling participants what data will be collected, how it will be stored, and what ultimate outputs will be created (which usually means articles and books). But in the private sector, it is not entirely knowable beforehand how and in what ways the data will be used. In a typical organization, market research findings are routinely shared throughout the organization and (with any luck!) for years to come. It is difficult for ethnographers to envision the potential future uses of all the data they will collect, much less to explain all these potential uses to participants in a way they may truly understand. So informed consent means explaining to participants that their faces and likenesses will be shared with members of the client organization in various formats including, but not limited to, audio, video, still photographs, and written field note summaries. Some ethnographers choose to always use participant code names for this very reason, because attaching a name to a video and suddenly having that video shared with an entire company may represent a clear potential for harm, depending on the topic of research. To avoid this trouble, ethnographers can either avoid taking photographs of faces or always rely on code names, or both.

The final difference is how private-sector ethnographers grapple with what Cefkin (2009) calls "moral and political complicity" with the pursuit of profit. Since the very practice of private-sector ethnography involves generating gain for oneself and one's clients, private-sector ethnographers can focus on this issue as a means of ethical practice. They may follow Hammershoy and Madsen's (2012) argument that "Do no harm" is far too low a bar for business anthropologists. They argue that private-sector ethnographers should aspire to actively do good, which goes far beyond the burden of simply mitigating harm to participants and being transparent. They argue that the very notion of a universal moral principle of "harm" is too ambiguous in the first place. The dynamic nature of business anthropology means that moral principles unfold in particular situations, with unique and sometimes ambiguous meanings. It cannot be universally determined, for example, that market-based applications of ethnography are always "evil," because there is no universal moral principle of what evil actually is. Carol Gilligan (1993) famously argued that the very idea of an abstract morality, decontextualized from real relationships and real situations, is a fundamentally gendered conception of morality in the first place. For Gilligan, morality is always contextual. Hammershoy and Madsen apply this principle to private-sector ethnography by exhorting anthropologists to ask themselves, "Is this fundamentally a good project? [Am] I being as truthful to it as humanly possible?" (2012, p. 81). The most ethical private-sector ethnographic practice is the ability to "stay honest" throughout the project.

An Ethical Hypothetical: The Issue of Deceit

Imagine a situation in which an ethnographer finds that a potentially malicious or deceitful course of action could be quite profitable for the client. For example, imagine the ethnographer is studying the experiences of individuals with a chronic illness that limits their mobility. The client's product is a health product, but not one generally used to treat depression. Suppose the ethnographer discovers that this kind of patient tends to use consumer products as a way of masking his depression, brought on by this illness. Any product could fill this consumer's emptiness, but the client's product is especially well positioned to be attractive to the consumer. It appears to be health-related, and it satisfies that need the patient has to fill his emptiness with consumer purchases.

What can an ethnographer do with this information? Hiding the name of the company, in this case, is just the beginning of potentially malicious deceitful actions the ethnographer could take.

There are essentially two courses of action. The ethnographer can present this finding as a potential strategy for selling more products, with or without the proviso that it may be unethical to exploit a consumer's depression for the purposes of profit. This general approach frames the participant's depression, fundamentally, as an opportunity. The ethnographer's ethical proviso may or may not be ignored by the client, and the ethnographer fails to take a moral position about whether this "opportunity" is ethical. In this first course of action, an opportunistic company might exploit the patient's vulnerability in marketing and communications. Slogans might hint at depression without saying it. Advertising copy might suggest the product's ability to alleviate depression, without directly making such a claim. The ethnographer is complicit with this morally bankrupt course of action because he failed to offer a moral position.

The second course of action, by contrast, problematizes the patient's depression as a cultural phenomenon. The ethnographer could argue that the cultural impact of framing depression as an "opportunity" is a morally wrong position to take. Consider describing the patient as a person caught in a maelstrom of existential challenges. He finds himself without control over his day-to-day life. His bodily movements are not under his control, which threatens his very autonomy as an individual. This product can be a way the patient copes with this lack of autonomy. Buying the client's product is a symbolic act of reclaiming autonomy that his illness has compromised. The ethnographer would suggest, in this second course of action, that the patient needs some form of redemption. The patient's depression is not framed as an "opportunity" to exploit, but as the essence of his lived experience. In the first course of action, the ethnographer offers the company a path to exploitation and profit; in the second, he offers the company a path to empathy with real people's pain.

In this second course of action, the company might choose to "stay honest," and tell potential consumers that its product does not treat depression or the chronic illness. The company truthfully suggests that its product offers some comfort to people who are experiencing the depressive symptoms from this chronic illness—a way to feel just a little bit better. If the company "stays honest," consumers will see that the company truly understands their experience, and they may reward the company with their business—and perhaps more importantly, their loyalty—because they feel understood. They are not deceived into thinking their depression will go away, but they feel comforted that at least this company has an idea of what it's like living with this particular illness.

The distinction is a subtle one, but it centers around the question of deceit. An ethnographer can be a party to deceit, or she can "stay honest" and offer the client ways to engage in market activity that is ethical. In this case, the ethnographer can raise the question, what values would the company embody were it to offer products in either of these ways? What kinds of consumers would it attract? What kinds of employees and suppliers? By painting the opportunity space as an arena in which a company's lived values translate into brand, the ethnographer presents moral questions in terms of company culture. It makes the situation intelligible to clients and stakeholders, but even better, it allows them to debate morality within the company-sanctioned topic of brand and brand equity. Few organizations allow patently moral conversations to happen.

A Special Note about Children

I almost never do research with children, mostly because I study adult practices of productivity and consumer behavior. Some researchers specialize in children's culture or behavior, however, which requires a higher level of ethical commitment. Research has shown that children have a difficult time differentiating between advertising and other types of content, and even understanding the purpose of advertising itself (Oates, Blades, and Gunter, 2002). Since children's cognitive development is simply not the same as adults', it behooves private-sector ethnographers to take special care with children. Parents' consent is not only legally required in most jurisdictions, but it is morally required if ethnographers are to follow the tenet of transparency. Moreover, studies designed to uncover marketing strategies for children must consider the harm they do to children. Building more interesting and better toys is one thing, but taking advantage of children's cognitive development for the purposes of profit is entirely another. Because children are so susceptible to marketing, I decided that I would not participate in any studies designed to market or advertise to children.

Ethical Practice Audits

Ethical ethnographic practice is entirely possible in the private sector. Ethnographers can and should be aware of how their work differs from that of their academic colleagues. They should also be able to clearly articulate to those colleagues what steps they take to ensure ethical practice. Regular audits of ethical practice are conducted in academia through the institutional review boards (IRBs) that approve the ethics of research proposals. Few private-sector organizations have anything similar to these audits, but not because they're impossible. Regular ethical audits are simply not part of many business functions. It is in this way that ethical practice must become cultural. For yourself, commit to reviewing regularly your own ethical practice. Enroll colleagues in this process, especially if they are ethnographers. Involve yourself in communities such as AnthroDesign and EPIC. Decide what is non-negotiable for you. Rate yourself on your follow-through to those ethical commitments.

In the end, ethnographers and journalists alike can get away with unethical practice. There are many prominent examples from which we can choose. There are many recent examples of academic researchers faking data, including the incredible story of Diederik Stapel, the Dutch psychologist who faked social research data for decades before finally being caught, fired, and publicly humiliated. He recently told the *New York Times* why it took him so long to get caught: "Everybody wants you to be novel and creative, but you also need to be truthful and likely. You need to be able to say that this is completely new and exciting, but it's very likely given what we know so far" (Bhattacharjee, 2013). In other words, our clients and stakeholders expect us to find something unusual, interesting, or even exotic. It is tempting to give them what they expect. But the role of the ethnographer is not to entertain or titillate, and certainly not to strong-arm or intimidate participants. The ethnographer is there to witness, inquire after, and analyze culture. There is nothing in that endeavor that is antithetical to ethical practice.

Chapter 7
Sampling

"He interviewed 10,000 young people," my colleague recently told me, as he held up a copy of Don Tapscott's *Grown Up Digital*. My colleague was so impressed with the number that he cited the sample size and not any of the actual research findings.

Ten thousand people does indeed sound impressive. But as you read more closely you realize that it's not 10,000 "interviews," but 10,000 young people having filled out a survey, and the vast majority of them did it by themselves in front of a computer without any researcher there to "interview" them. The researchers only visited 30 individuals and spoke with them face-to-face. There's a big difference between 10,000 and 30.

The problem with phrases like "10,000 interviews" is that they set the expectation of what is humanly possible far too high for even the most generous budgets or timelines. These numbers come to be normative. In other words, just like Mike Holmes, Don Tapscott sets the bar on what we should expect. Just like Mike Holmes, Tapscott has entirely different priorities than I do. As a private-sector ethnographer, I am interested in a deep understanding of the nature and context of products and services. Tapscott is more concerned with macro-level patterns of the entire population. His claim of 10,000 interviews skews the standard of what's expected or even possible. The worst part, however, is that it's not even necessary! Tapscott's findings would have been just as legitimate if he

Practical Ethnography: A Guide to Doing Ethnography in the Private Sector by Sam Ladner, 101–113. © 2014 Left Coast Press, Inc. All rights reserved.

had simply interviewed his 30 young people in their homes or offices. His findings might have had a slightly different focus, but they would still have been worth reading.

How is that possible? Let me explain.

This chapter is about sampling. Sampling, at its heart, is a shortcut. If you had time to ask everyone in the country the same questions, you would actually be conducting a census. That's what "census" means— asking absolutely everybody. But censuses are time consuming and terribly expensive, so they're not done very often. Samples are a way to do research without that time and expense. What most people don't realize is that large samples are not always necessary, and good samples aren't always random. In fact, sometimes random sampling simply is the worst way you can spend your research budget.

The sampling problem that ethnographers often grapple with is that clients and stakeholders are influenced by the normativity of large sample sizes. The Don Tapscotts of the world have trained them to believe "prediction" of patterns is the goal of research. Certainly, there is value in predicting patterns. Unfortunately, it has become the *only* thing that most people expect from social research. Prediction is flat, lacking in texture, nuance, and deep understanding. Predicting patterns, when coupled with interpretation, is the gold standard of research practice, but it's very common to settle for prediction alone. Our clients seek large sample sizes because they believe they are answering the central research question: what will happen? It is our job to offer them another research question: What does this mean? When you remove probability as a meaningful exemplar, and you abandon the promise of prediction, large random samples are expensive and ineffective. Instead, your job as an ethnographer is to find participants who offer the greatest potential for understanding the phenomenon at hand. Sampling, for the ethnographer, is not an enterprise in accurate prediction, but an attempt to offer explanation. Unfortunately, many of our clients and stakeholders have little familiarity with explanation, which is both a challenge and an opportunity. We can offer them deep insight that they've never received before, but we must also manage their expectations away from prediction and only prediction.

The Logic of Sampling

To explain, let me describe some of the assumptions that go into research methods. Quantitative researchers have a set of assumptions that are often unspoken but have been taken up by the general population without a lot of thought or reflection. My aim here is to reveal the logic behind these assumptions, to allow private-sector ethnographers to make informed, thoughtful decisions about their samples. I must note that this is not a complete chapter on quantitative sampling methodology and will not prepare you to create robust, quantitative samples. But it will inform you about why 10,000 interviews are unnecessary for ethnographic study.

First, quantitative researchers assume that their topic can be modeled after random events. That's what would happen if you flipped a coin. Heads for yes, and tails for no. We know a great deal about random events, and we can model them very precisely. These models have more predictive power as the number of events increases. The more times you flip a coin, the more accurate your prediction. If I flip a coin three times, you probably won't accurately predict how many heads will come up. But if I flip it 1,000 times? You'd probably guess much more accurately how many heads would come up. After all, there are only two choices; you would guess 500 heads and 500 tails. So if you end up with 800 heads and 200 tails, you know there is something else going on. Is the coin loaded in some way? Does it favor heads over tails? Probably.

The second key assumption quantitative researchers make is that they can introduce random logic through sampling. The sampling method plays a very important role in this line of thinking. The quantitative researcher employs some form of randomness in her sampling, assuming that this act will set the stage for her results to possibly be random. As you can imagine, probability sampling is quite time consuming, requires a high level of skill, and can be very expensive. But it is the only way researchers can confidently compare their results to purely random results.

Now here's the funny part: qualitative researchers don't care about comparing their results to random results. As a result, they don't tend to care about probability sampling.

Qualitative researchers start with an entirely different set of assumptions. First, they reject the assertion that social events can ever be truly random in the first place. People are not like molecules or atoms; they are

Figure 2: Assumptions in Quantitative and Qualitative Sampling

Quantitative	Qualitative
We want to generalize to the population.	People are not predictable like random events.
⬇	⬇
Random events are predictable.	Random events are irrelevant to social life.
⬇	⬇
We can compare our results to purely random ones.	Probability sampling is expensive and inefficient.
Therefore...	**Therefore...**
Probability sampling is the best choice.	Non-probability sampling is the best choice.

sentient beings who make decisions and interpretations about the world around them. Because of this, there is no such thing as purely random events involving people. It would be absurd to even consider randomness as a potential model for social life. There is nothing random about it. Moreover, qualitative researchers are not primarily interested in prediction. They do not set out to predict if the population at large might use a particular smartphone app. They're more interested in meaning and human expression. Former stock trader and current author Nassim Taleb sums up this view nicely: "No matter how many dollars are spent on research, predicting revolutions is not the same as counting cards; humans will never be able to turn politics and economics into the intractable randomness of blackjack" (2012).

For this reason, qualitative researchers do not compare their results to purely random ones and therefore have no need of probability sampling. You could go further and argue that qualitative researchers do not need large sample sizes at all, but that would not be entirely correct. Qualitative researchers do want to understand patterns of events, but they do not necessarily want to offer prediction. How do working-class boys become working-class men? This is the question Paul Willis asked when he observed young people in the classroom and interviewed them about their experiences for his book, *Learning to Labour* (1981). He was certainly looking for an amount of data large enough to discern some variations or patterns, but he made no claims as to how many working-class boys would definitively become working-class men. He needed enough data to draw conclusions, but at no time did he need any sort of randomness, and probability theory had no bearing on his sample size. It made sense for him to observe an entire year in the classroom to see how seasons change and boys come to occupy certain roles. But he was never concerned with randomly choosing sufficient numbers of students. Why would a qualitative researcher go to the expense and trouble of probability sampling if there is no value in comparing his results to random results? He would not, and he does not. Qualitative researchers tend to select their participants based on the needs of the study.

Perhaps the qualitative researcher wants to know how physicians use smartphone apps. She would not go to the trouble of randomly selecting physicians, who are difficult to recruit in the first place. Instead, she would create a set of recruitment criteria that are relevant to the research question. Perhaps she only wants to study cancer specialists, so she recruits only oncologists. She also wants to make sure they have a smartphone, and perhaps even a variety of models. She may wish to see different types of clinics, and app use may differ from site to site. She probably would want to meet different types of oncologists as well, some old, some young, some men, some women, some pediatric, some geriatric. But she would not go to the trouble of randomly selecting hundreds of physicians. The ethnographer, unlike the survey researcher, isn't just sampling people— she is also sampling sites, times, and seasons.

What Kinds of Samples Do Ethnographers Take?

Private-sector ethnographers sample many more than the 12 people that is typical in a short, private-sector study. They do not simply sample people; they sample times, locations, seasons, working conditions, family photos, home design—the list is potentially endless. In a typical private-sector study, an ethnographer is seeking what Anselem Strauss and Barney Glaser call "saturation," or the point at which you begin to hear the same information repeated. When you are *no longer surprised by the responses* you are getting, this is when saturation starts. When you are *tired of hearing* what your respondents are telling you, you have achieved saturation. This may happen with as few as five participants in a very focused, user-experience type of study, as Jacob Nielsen and others (2006) have argued. But for more anthropologically informed studies, which are wider in scope, saturation often begins at eight or nine participants. It is common in private-sector studies for saturation to occur around 11 or 12 participants.

"But How Many People Did You Talk To?"

Interviewing 12 people does not mean your sample includes "only 12 participants." It includes 12 locations, 12 groups (families, work teams), and all the objects and tools within those 12 locations. One useful way to think of your sample is to keep track of how many data points you collected. In my last study I completed, I interviewed 19 key informants. That sounds like a fair number, but it's certainly not 10,000. However, I visited 26 separate locations, interviewed an additional 12 people serendipitously, took 598 photographs, recorded 1,200 minutes of video and 28 hours of audio. Suddenly, my data set looks a lot larger than simply "19

Table 4: Data Points Collected in a Recent Workplace Ethnography

Participants			
Owners	Employees	Others	
19	10	2	
Data Collection			
Photographs	Hours of observation	Minutes of video	
598	62.1	1264	
Locations			
Home office	Startup office	Co-working space	Total
7	11	8	26

key informants." I did not sample only key informants, but everything and everybody that was around them.

Private-sector ethnographers may not have large numbers of people, but they will have large numbers of items in their samples. They may not have a probability sample, and therefore cannot predict how their findings relate to the general population, but they will be able to discern patterns and themes.

Selecting the Ethnographic Sample: The Sampling Frame

The sample is typically drawn from a list called the sampling frame. Finding the sampling frame is by far the most challenging part of sampling for either qualitative or quantitative research. Ever wonder why so many studies involve university students? It's because there is a ready sampling frame in every university: the class lists of all courses. Outside the university, there is no such list.

The private sector does offer some solutions to this problem. Professional recruitment companies typically have lists of potential participants. They assemble these lists over years of asking consumers if they'd like to participate in research studies. There are usually several problems with these lists. First, there is definitely a systematic difference between those that opt in and those that do not. It is ideal to have a selection of real people who are simply living their lives and forming opinions about products and services. Unfortunately, the people who opt in are not this kind of person. They have actively chosen to take part in market research, which sometimes means they become what the industry calls "professional respondents." They lack authenticity and in the worst cases provide falsely positive opinions about any product or service because they believe this is what you want to hear. I personally have had my share of professional respondents, and they do make the ethnographic research agenda very difficult to realize. But perhaps the worst problem with recruitment company lists is that they are not designed for ethnography. Typically, the people who opt into to these lists believe they will attend focus group sessions in a room with a two-way mirror and free pizza on the way in. Ethnography necessarily means contextual research, so many of these participants are taken aback when you suggest coming to their home or office. They did not sign up for this!

Despite these shortcomings, professional recruitment lists can provide you what you need to begin your study. You should give careful instructions to the recruiters about ethnography and how it differs, and to make it extra clear to participants what they can expect from the experience. Consider offering a "comfort call" to the participants the day before the field visit, telling them what to expect

There are alternatives to professional recruitment companies. Social media offers a new avenue to recruit participants that does not require a professional recruitment company, but it does require social-media savvy, a web site, and a dedicated recruiter. Twitter, Facebook, and LinkedIn all offer great opportunities to recruit qualified participants. But one cannot simply join a social network and expect to use it as a recruitment tool immediately. To leverage these networks, recruiters should look for what sociologist Mark Granovetter (1973) famously called "weak ties," or people outside your closest friends and family. Your former co-workers or members of your high-school class are two excellent examples of weak ties, which Granovetter demonstrated are more likely to help people find job opportunities than are "strong ties." Researchers have recently found that Facebook users who get the most benefit out of their Facebook network are those who make a point of staying in touch and sending direct messages to Facebook friends from time to time (Burke and Kraut, 2011). The key to using social media for recruiting, therefore, is maintaining your network through direct engagement with other users. Obviously, this requires a long-term commitment and a regular, concerted approach to using online social networks.

Of course, this approach would be inappropriate if your goal was to recruit participants who are not web- or tech-savvy. But because you are not creating a probability sample, you have every reason to use these tools. You must ensure that you have an anonymous avenue for potential participants to contact you, such as an input form on your web site and not a "please 'like' this if you want to participate!" on Facebook. A simple email link will also suffice. In both cases, however, you should make clear what you will and will not do with email addresses (see Chapter 6, "Ethical Ethnography").

Figure 3: Types of Participants to Recruit

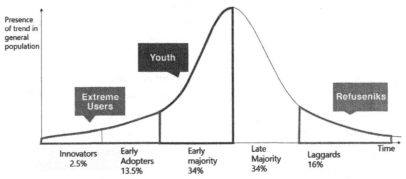

Adapted from Rogers (1995).

Selecting the Ethnographic Sample

Just because you are not interested in a probability sample does not mean you need not be systematic in your recruitment. Ethnographers may not recruit random samples, but they certainly do spend time and effort in recruiting well. The primary concern in ethnographic sampling is to gain access to participants' contexts, and from there, derive insight about their attitudes, values, and beliefs and more deeply understand a particular product space.

The type of truth we are seeking with ethnography is not the predictive kind of truth, but the deep insight, or what Geertz called "thick description." Sociologist Max Weber called this truth *verstehen*, or deep understanding. Let's imagine you are researching ovens and cooking, in order to build a better oven. You are working with industrial designers and perhaps engineers to create a new and better oven. What do you need to know about ovens? Who can help you find it out?

An ethnographer would need to know what role the oven plays in domestic cooking. What role does the oven play in everyday cooking? How do everyday meals fit or not fit with the metaphor of the oven? How do cooks use the oven? What are the must-have functions of an oven?

You can answer these questions by recruiting two types of participants. The first is the type of participant who is the average, garden variety cook. There is nothing extreme about this person. He may use the oven a few times a week and be well versed enough to have an opinion on it.

This kind of person would give you the general lay of the land of everyday cooking. The other kind of participant is the extreme user. This can be either the "alpha chef" of the household who routinely puts on large dinner parties using Julia Child's recipes. Or it can be the "refusnik," who will not use the oven for any type of cooking. Both of these extreme users (or non-users, as the case may be) will tell you what "normal" is. They are the influencers that set the tone for the middle-of-the-road cooks. Alpha Chefs may explain what an average cook would aspire to be, while Refusniks will tell you what an average cook would avoid if at all possible. The average and the extreme are wonderful examples to have in your sample.

I once had a project for a client that involved ethnographic observations of older men in their doctors' offices. I recommended observing "average," regular, everyday patients. But then I also suggested we recruit

What I Learned from a Refusnik

Recently, I had a Refusnik in my sample, completely by accident. I was looking for self-employed, tech-savvy startup owners or founders. This particular participant turned out to be a full-time employee who cared little about his technology and simply used whatever his company gave him. I despaired when I arrived at what was supposed to be his home office (it was just his house). I quickly realized that he was anything but the extreme early-adopter I was looking for. But then it occurred to me that he was a Refusnik, and I could test some of my emerging hypotheses about technology use with him. The self-employed people were very strategic and active in their technology choices; this participant was quite passive and uninvolved. The self-employed people expected their technology to produce meaningful, actionable data about their own productivity; this participant paid little attention to what simple metrics were available by default. Where the self-employed used technology as an expression of their own autonomy, this full-time employee experienced technology as something foisted upon him, like the other conditions of his working experience. Through interviewing this Refusnik, I was able to analyze some of my emergent themes in a way that I might never have been able to otherwise. Refusnisks give you this opportunity.

patients at a practice that caters to gay men. The reason behind this was to see how masculinity functions. If we saw the straight men asking qualitatively different questions than the gay men, we would know something important about how they see themselves and their sexual identities. As a bonus, we would have a dataset of interest to understand a niche market, the gay market. My client understood my logic, but in the end did not opt for recruiting gay patients. To this day I wish I could have convinced her! I am certain we would have learned important insights about what it means to be a man in today's world.

In order to get the "typical" and the "extreme" participants, private-sector ethnographers typically create a recruitment screener, just as do focus group moderators and even survey researchers. Private-sector ethnographers attempt to encode their desired typical and extreme participants into the sample in reasonable proportions. Going back to our oven example, this would mean asking potential participants about how often they cook using the oven. The recruiter would aim to gather a significant portion of "average" cooks, and then some "extreme" alpha chefs and refusniks. These participants should also have a few other characteristics that are relevant to the study, such as having a kitchen with a functioning stove, having a family to cook for, or whatever is most relevant to the study.

Household income level is one recruitment criterion which reveals our hidden assumptions about economic class. We tend to ignore or silence people who earn less money, under the assumption that their opinions or buying patterns do little to help our business. That assumption is usually wrong. Lower-income consumers are underserved and in fact represent a great untapped market. This is particularly true in financial services. Just in America, about 10 percent of Americans are what researchers call "unbanked," or without any basic banking services, such as savings accounts or check cashing (The Federal Reserve Bank, 2001). This number is often much, much higher in developing nations, meaning that there is a massive, under-served population and a business model. Micro-finance is one way to offer financial services to this population, but large banks eschewed this approach until Nobel Prize winner Muhammad Yunis showed that you can actually earn more money for this kind of lending. He began lending small amounts of money to very poor women and charging them interest. His Grameen Bank makes money while at the same time making a positive impact on the world. Now large banks like Citibank have micro-finance divisions, which lend smaller amounts at a higher rate of return. Participants often span gender, ethnicity, and income level. But what I find often in the private sector is that commissioners of research frequently decline to interview people of lower socio-economic status under the mistaken belief that their opinions are not relevant.

A marketer may assume that someone with less than $40,000 in household income cannot afford to buy a stove. But what they do not realize is that this person has a valid opinion and is part of our greater culture. Her ideas about what cooking is about will tell us more about cooking in general. Moreover, she may even offer ideas specific to lower-income consumers. All too often, businesses dismiss those with lower incomes as "poor customers," without realizing that innovation can emerge from understanding the breadth of human experience. This is one of the key advantages ethnography has to offer the private sector, one which survey research often fails to provide.

Ethnographic Samples Can Never Offer Prediction

Ethnographers cannot offer what their quantitative colleagues can: prediction of what will happen. You will find yourself to be tempted to offer the smallest of predictions because of the questions your clients and stakeholders will ask. "Should we build this app?" "Is this the right design?" "Are we hitting the right demographic?" These questions are all implicitly asking, "Can you guarantee me that your results are a reasonable representation of the population at large?" You may never answer this question with anything other than: "These results are not generalizable."

But remember that your job is to show your clients and stakeholders that prediction is a poor substitute for deep understanding. You may never know if this is the "right design," even if you had limitless time and budget; some research questions can never be answered. Instead of obsessing over making the "wrong" choice, your clients and stakeholders must be given enough deep understanding that they forget to wonder if it is the "right" design. Instead, they have the confidence that they really know their customers and their needs. They can hold the bold assertion that it *is* the right design because they have really understood where current designs have failed. They are unconcerned with hitting the "right demographic" because they know their product is designed so well that the right people will buy it, use it, and love it. When people ask prediction questions of ethnographic data, they are not asking research questions at all. They are asking fearful questions. They are demonstrating indecision and lack of confidence. Ethnographic sampling, when hitting saturation, will empower clients and give them the confidence to triumph over their indecision. This is the beauty of ethnography: it gives such rich understanding of people and everyday lives that business people often forget to ask prediction questions. For this reason, sampling may first appear to be your biggest research problem, but it is, in fact, not a large problem.

Chapter 8
Fieldwork

I was almost 23 when I decided it was a good idea to start playing rugby. My friend Karen and I had seen a poster advertising a women's rugby team at our university. At the time, it was very unusual for a women's rugby team to even exist. Perhaps it was for this reason that Karen and I joined the team. The captain of the team was an athletic woman named Sharon, who was doing her master's degree in pharmacy, which involved some sort of complex laboratory work. It might have been her scientific prowess, or perhaps that she was almost six feet tall, but I found Sharon to be far more competent, strong, and just plain better than I was. I congratulated myself heavily for making it through my very first game without a broken bone.

In the surprisingly terrifying moments before our second game, Sharon gathered the troops. "You should have game jitters," she said. I felt comforted. "Not the 'Oh my God, I'm actually playing rugby jitters,'" she cautioned, "but just regular game jitters." I blanched. I was sure I still had the "Oh my God, I'm actually playing rugby jitters."

Fieldwork jitters are a little like rugby jitters. It doesn't matter how many times I've gone into the field, how many interviews I've conducted, how many times I've gotten lost or been late to meet a participant, I still get fieldwork jitters. I don't get "Oh my God, I'm doing ethnography" jitters anymore, but just regular fieldwork jitters. This chapter is about the incredibly emotionally taxing practice of fieldwork. It is an attempt

Practical Ethnography: A Guide to Doing Ethnography in the Private Sector by Sam Ladner, 115–138. © 2014 Left Coast Press, Inc. All rights reserved.

to prepare you for what to do in the field. I will give you a list of things to do and things *not* to do, and nuggets of advice. But absolutely nothing can prepare you for the sheer panic you experience upon hearing a threatening sound from under the hood of your rental car as you drive, without a functioning GPS, in some area loosely known as "Upstate New York." Or the dreadful realization that your participant really doesn't speak English, much less read a daily English newspaper four to five times a week, as your recruitment company had assured you. Or the squirm-worthy moment when a participant proudly shows off his own art and you smile and nod like an idiot. Unlike survey researchers, ethnographers find themselves physically in the middle of all sorts of situations. It's impossible for them to escape squirm-worthy moments because that is precisely what ethnography is made up of. The ethnographer's job is to experience every panicky, dreadful, and squirmy moment and record it.

In this chapter, I'll describe how to prepare for the fieldwork phase of your research, as well as for individual fieldwork visits. I'll describe the typical elements of an applied ethnography field study, and what you should aspire to do and achieve while in the field. I will also describe what you should be doing on the "home front" once you return from your fieldwork (note that I will describe actual analysis in the next chapter).

No matter how many times you read this chapter, you will never be truly prepared. Fieldwork is a tacit skill, an embodied experience. Recall Hubert Dreyfus's (2009) contention that no other experience can rival the transformational impact of face-to-face interaction.[1] This book is not a substitute for actual fieldwork. You will have the "Oh my God, I'm doing ethnography" jitters for your first or even your sixth project. But after awhile, they will become regular fieldwork jitters. This book will not allow you to skip the step of learning how to do fieldwork.

What Is "Fieldwork"?

What is an ethnographer actually doing when she goes into the field? Certainly she is physically locating herself in the same place as her participants. She is collecting data in the form of photographs and notes. She is interviewing participants. She is observing. But these are just activities. What is the notion of "fieldwork"?

Fieldwork is two things. First, it is the ethnographer acting as a research instrument. Just like a survey questionnaire, or a focus-group video camera, the ethnographer herself collects all the data. Second, fieldwork is the symbolic act of "walking in the shoes" of your participants. By physically going to another location, the ethnographer is leaving behind that which she knows and, in some cases, controls. She is becoming a member of her participants' world and choosing willfully to follow their rules and adopt their ways. This is the critical step of establishing rapport. Rapport underpins qualitative research generally, but ethnography in particular. These twin activities are what differentiates ethnographic fieldwork from other research experiences and it is what is so cognitively and emotionally draining about ethnography.

The ethnographer is both an instrument and a professional guest. She is constantly collecting data by noticing things and interpreting them on the fly. She is conscious of the participants' norms and behaviors, duly notes them as additional data, while at the same time she attempts to adopt those behaviors herself. In practice, this means the ethnographer is concentrating and thinking several steps ahead throughout her time in the field. It is extremely taxing. An ethnographer goes to a particular time and place and interacts with the people (and pets!) in that place. She is a visitor in that place, but she must do more than merely be a visitor. She must establish trust with her participants, and this rapport will allow her to understand what is significant to them. She is practicing "procedures for counting to one" (Van Maanen, Manning, and Miller, 1986), which involves sifting through all that is happening and instantly understanding whether it is germane to her topic. She is a human instrument which detects significance and records it, in a note, a video recording, or a photograph. She must make snap judgments as to what is relevant about that time and place. She must act like a visitor, but function as a human instrument. This fine balance is very hard to effect.

In her ethnography of life in Flin Flon, Manitoba, Meg Luxton (1980) spent countless hours at kitchen tables interviewing participants. In between drinking coffee, lending a hand to watch children, and breathing in second-hand smoke, Luxton was formulating a theory about what work in the home is all about. She was also establishing a trust with her participants that was critical. She was embedded in the chaos of everyday life with small children, but she constantly returned to her research agenda while being there. She returned to her rented house in Flin Flon to go through her notes and search for connections. The next day, she may have found herself in the grocery store and realized that she should watch what people were buying because her participants had explained how important their grocery shopping skills were to the running of the household. In the end, she devoted an entire chapter to the skill of grocery shopping, which is not something that could have arisen from a survey or a focus group. It could only emerge by being there, in the grocery store, and thinking about her research agenda. Luxton was constantly on the lookout for ideas about domestic labor, even when she herself was performing domestic labor.

Gaining (and Keeping) Access

Ethnography does not happen without access to participants' contexts. This is why the recruitment phase is so important. Private-sector ethnographers can underestimate the subtle social reciprocity of gaining access because they usually pay participants for their time. But payment alone is not enough to ensure access is *true* access; being polite, respecting your participants' space and time, and guarding ethical practice carefully must also be on the ethnographer's mind. Getting and keeping access adds an entirely new layer of difficulty in ethnographic practice. Staying aware of your research agenda while being physically in your participants' context is indeed difficult. But maintaining an even keel while in the field is also critical in order to ensure you will continue to get access to your participants.

Fieldwork can be extremely draining, and ethnographers occasionally lose their tempers, as J. L. Briggs (1970) did during her fieldwork in the Canadian Arctic. Briggs angrily confronted a white man from outside the Inuit community over a canoe that belonged to the Inuit. Much to her surprise, the Inuit community was offended by her angry outburst and ostracized her for an agonizing three months. Her entire project would have been lost had she not been able to regain access to the community. Private-sector ethnographers may not experience as dramatic an incident as this, but they can certainly experience moments when participants feel disrespected.

Gaining access doesn't end when participants agree to participate. It is an ongoing task for the ethnographer. John Seeley (Seeley, Sim, and Loosely,1956) had a team of colleagues and research assistants work for five years in Toronto's north end, attending parent meetings at schools, interviewing families in their homes, and spending time inside classrooms with children. Throughout the ethnographic project, Seeley and his colleagues needed to ensure that these parents and teachers would continue to allow them access to their homes, their schools, and their children. This is perhaps why data collection lasted as long as it did; the research team took baby steps in order not to upset the fine balance of the community. Not only were researchers focusing on collecting data while in the field, they were also focusing on keeping the lines of access open.

As Briggs's and Seeley's work suggests, one key determinant of how difficult ethnography can be is getting access. Some ethnographers are unable to gain access without becoming "covert" ethnographers. In academic ethnography, covert fieldwork exists and is conducted after rigorous ethics reviews. It is increasingly difficult to conduct covert fieldwork in academia, partly due to the high bar of approval by institutional review boards, but also because ethnographers themselves are choosing not to "go undercover" for various practical and ethical reasons.

In private-sector ethnography, covert ethnography is virtually indefensible. As I argued in Chapter 6, private-sector ethnographers face a far bigger threat to ensuring their own ethical conduct than do academic ethnographers. They must recognize that the very idea that these data will be used to sell things itself presents a moral quandary. Selling things to people is not, in itself, a moral breach. After all, some of the purest forms of human expression are market-based activities. Any artificial line we tend to draw between the market and the supposedly "purer" social life is largely imaginary (Zelizer, 2007). But what *does* cross the line is the intent to deceive for purposes of selling things. Therein lies the very problem of covert ethnography in the private sector. By its very definition, covert ethnography to sell things contravenes this moral principle of avoiding deceit and cannot, therefore, be morally defensible. Your ethical conduct as a private-sector ethnography means that you must clearly inform participants of the nature of the ethnography. This cannot be done with covert ethnography.

What Ethnography Is Not

Paco Underhill conducts one common form of covert market research that is often mistaken for ethnography. In his book, *Why We Buy*, Underhill explains how he and his researchers observe shoppers in stores and take careful notes about key variables in store design. Underhill's famous contribution is the "butt brush," or the accidental touching of a person's backside against a shelf behind them. Underhill's research has revealed that the "butt brush" will almost always mean a shopper will not buy in that store. Underhill's method is covert in the sense that shoppers do not know they are, and have not consented to, being observed (incidentally, the shop workers and their consent is not discussed in Underhill's book). But his work cannot be called ethnography for several reasons. First, it is not focused on cultural explanation, but simply on descriptions of shopping behavior. Second, Underhill's research is "non-reactive," meaning it is simply the passive collection of data without any interaction with participants to ask for clarification or opinion. Observation is indeed an ethnographic method, but in ethnography it is complemented by clarifying questions and sit-down interviews. Watching customers walk up and down store aisles is only part of the cultural phenomenon of shopping, and Underhill's methods do not include interviewing participants, or even following them to other stores, much less spending time with them and understanding their worldviews and experiences. There is no attempt to "walk in the shoes" of shoppers, simply to follow them around individual stores. Underhill's work is "fieldwork" in the sense that this work takes place "in the field" of various retail locations, but it is not ethnographic fieldwork. There is no emic position nor cultural lens.

Another emergent form of market research that is falsely referred to as ethnography is the passive collection of video interactions in private places. Researchers place video cameras in particular locations and simply record what happens. Some of my clients from the pharmaceutical industry, in particular, have asked me about sales pitches that purport to be selling "ethnography," but really are simply selling analysis of video-recorded interactions. My clients have been legitimately confused by these sales pitches because what they describe doesn't sound like anything I might have done for them. In this "ethnography," the research company places a video camera in a physician's office and observes interactions between doctors and patients. The research company then purports to analyze these interactions and produce a report.

There is so much wrong with this approach that it's hard to know where to start. First, it is covert for commercial purposes. It's unlikely that the patients truly understand what the purpose of this research is, given that no researcher is ever actually there. Whether they sign a consent form is somewhat irrelevant; it's not an *informed* consent because they have little idea of who the researcher is and what she'll do with the data. The research agenda is represented only by a camera, not a living, breathing researcher who can be quizzed, examined, and approved by the patient.

Second, when I do fieldwork in health care, I do not ever record video. Health care is such a personal and intimate experience (not to mention legally private) that a video camera clearly compromises that intimacy. In the United States, the health care law Health Insurance Portability and Accountability Act, known as HIPAA,[2] specifically states that health-care providers must protect patients from being identified when particular topics like health history or previous treatments. This kind of information is typically passed in regular physician-patient interactions, and video recordings of such interactions could easily reveal the patient's identity. It is often easier to be compliant with the law if you simply avoid recording altogether. Novice ethnographers often panic at the thought of no electronic tools to help them, but it is incredibly good practice to rely solely on your own note-taking ability.

Fieldwork means being visible to your participant and following his lead and wishes. It's impossible to do that when you are not even physically there! Fieldwork, then, means you must be there, act as the primary research "instrument," and navigate the complexities of being in your participants' context.

Passive observation *alone* is not ethnographic, but it can add value when used in concert with interviewing and participating in a given activity. A video recording of a private place presents deep ethical problems, but it also does not give the ethnographer a "feel" for the place. The camera is an immovable eye that can only capture what is in its view. The ethnographer, by contrast, can move around, change perspectives, and overhear events happening "off camera."

Getting Ready

Getting ready to go into the field means preparing for the unknown. As former United States Secretary of Defense Donald Rumsfeld famously told us, there are "known unknowns" and "unknown unknowns." Unfortunately, in ethnographic fieldwork there are many "unknown unknowns." (My friend and colleague Steve Portigal has curated a collection of these "war stories" on his blog, *All This Chittah Chattah*. Novice ethnographers may find these stories informative, though be warned! These things actually happened!) How should one prepare for fieldwork?

Reading Around: Having a Theoretical Position

First, a robust and theoretically informed research design is critical. As I argued in Chapter 2, having a connection to some sort of theory, be it the presentation of self or the struggle to play the "appropriate" gender role, narrows your focus in the field. If you have a theoretical orientation before going into the field, you will know what to pay attention to and what to disregard. This is even more important for novice ethnographers; positively everything will look relevant your first few times in the field. So you must not skip this step of having a theoretically informed position. Contrary to popular opinion, spending time on theory actually shortens your time in the field and in analysis. Before you go into the field, spend some time leisurely "reading around." I use this vague phrase on purpose. Read books and articles that seem tangentially related to your general theoretical position.

Say, for example, you are about to do an ethnography of young men and their interest in video games. Your role is to collect insight about their attitudes and beliefs, but also very practical concerns like their aesthetic preferences and technological ecosystems. On the surface, this project does not appear to be specifically about gender roles. It may appear that these are young men doing what is "natural" for young men to do: play video games. But through your prior reading about gender, you will understand the "life project" these young men are engaged in necessarily involves grappling with masculinity and their emerging roles as men. Understanding their life project will help you design better products and services for them because you will have deep empathy and understanding about their struggles. In this case, you zero in on their struggle to become men.

You may read Nancy Chodorow's analysis of mothering (Chodorow, 1999) and realize that autonomy is something one must develop in contrast to one's same-sex parent. You may read Carole Pateman's argument that women cannot claim full citizenship because they don't have full rights to their bodies (Pateman, 1988), and from this you will understand that bodily autonomy is something young men use to signal their own autonomy. You may read Jung's analysis of the anima and how its feminine influence causes psychic stress in men (Jung, 1964). From this you may conclude that young men are both attracted to and recoil from their own femininity, which may explain why they occasionally choose a feminine avatar in game play. You may read Michael Kimmel's compelling work on young men's struggle to assert masculinity in their college years (Kimmel, 2008) and see that many young men want to be freed from the narrow gender role they've been given. None of these concepts on their face may seem directly relevant to what you're about to study. But they will spark ideas for you and prime you to observe important clues in the field. Once you have read around, you are ready to prepare practical concerns.

The Kit Ritual

You will need a "kit" to do fieldwork. Everyone's kit is slightly different, but they are all designed to do the same thing: help you collect data. My kit includes a digital still camera (fully charged!), a Livescribe digital recording pen and its notebook, my smartphone, blank informed consent forms, the participant's location and phone number written in several places, and my interview guide. In Chapter 4, "Ethnographic Tools," you'll find more information on what you can put in your kit. But as you prepare for field work, make sure you have your batteries fully charged, sufficient pages in your notebook, and sufficient space on your memory cards. Make this preparation a ritual.

The Kit Ritual is more than simply lining up your tools or writing down addresses. It is mental preparation. It is a quiet, focused meditation on your ethnographic agenda. Ethnographers who rush into the field without such a ritual will find themselves mentally unprepared for the first moments, and will need more time to adjust their mindset and

Defining Your Own 'Kit Ritual'

What should your own Kit Ritual look like? An ethnographer needs to be as relaxed and mentally clear as possible. After all, it is the ethnographer that is the primary research tool! Define your own Kit Ritual by identifying the main sources of potential distractions for you. I have colleagues who are "geographically challenged," and experience wayfinding as a stressful experience. If this sounds like you, mapping out the location ahead of time is probably the best way to alleviate anxiety and to prepare you to be focused while in the field. Ask yourself the following questions:

Question	Purpose
When I think about fieldwork, what makes me the most anxious?	Discover the source of your "Oh my god, I'm doing ethnography" jitters. If this is getting lost, spend time mapping. If it is forgetting your interview guide, memorize it. If it is social anxiety, visualize a smooth social interaction.
In the past, when I have had to think on my feet, what objects or tools gave me the comfort to do that well?	Ethnography is a tacit, embodied skill that requires quick thinking. Some circumstances may have helped you think quickly in the past, such as wearing comfortable shoes or having a pen ready-to-hand. Gather those items before fieldwork.
Thinking back to when I have performed poorly in a face-to-face meeting, what was the primary source of my poor performance?	We all have memories of the "epic fail" meetings. Thinking back to your epic fail, consider the source of your distraction. Were you too hungry? Did you show up late? Whatever set you off on the wrong path, develop a Kit Ritual that helps you avoid that situation.

become productive as researchers. During the Kit Ritual, I usually also review my interview guide, often by copying it out, by hand, into my notebook. This is my way of imprinting my research agenda onto my mind. It also helps me memorize the interview guide. By the time I finish copying out the interview guide, I have almost a muscle memory of what I need to do upon arrival. My last step in this ritual is reviewing how to find the location. Once you complete your pre-fieldwork ritual, it's time to get into the field.

Being There

Going into the field generally means interviewing and observing participants in their everyday life. In private-sector ethnography, the "participant observation" method is practiced almost exclusively, though there are examples of other methods. For example, in their work on "rapid assessment" in health care, Robert Trotter and his colleagues (2001) describe using several different methods, including surveys and impromptu focus groups of the community they are studying. In their method, the primary aim is to assess the effectiveness of health interventions, such as needle exchanges to prevent HIV transmission. This kind of ethnographic investigation is often beyond the budget of a typical ethnographic project. It entails a large team of researchers that are trained in multiple research methods, as well as statistical analysis software, assistants to perform data entry, and the ability to assemble and synchronize the research team's activities so that they are dedicated to this rapid assessment exclusively. Academic research teams can operate in this way, but private-sector research teams often face challenges in being dedicated to single projects for any length of time.

Sometimes "being there" is complemented well with "not being there," as was the case with David Randall's research into air-traffic control (ATC) processes. In their paper on fieldwork, David Randall, Richard Harper and Mark Rouncefield (2005) note that much of their knowledge of ATC processes stemmed from conversations and small talk that happened with participants *away from* the actual field site. They note that this was not *in situ* research at all, but it was inordinately valuable in helping them interpret what they did witness in the field. "Being there" should not fetishized as the only worthwhile research activity, therefore.

It is impossible to make good recommendations on ATC technology without witnessing and experiencing everyday life in the tower, but we should not forget that witnessing the site first-hand is not the only way to understand a field site.

Being there often means being patient. I once did an ethnography to help industrial designers innovate on traditional Christmas lights. In one participant's home, I literally crawled into the crawl space with her and sat on the basement's concrete floor as she proudly unwrapped her Christmas decorations. After about the eighth angel, my legs began to cramp and I somehow had to bring her back to talk about the lights in general. You must be patient in the field. When you visit a participant's house, and you are a guest. You must act like one.

This means from the very moment you arrive to the second you leave, you act as the most charming and easygoing dinner guest they've ever had. You are polite but not pushy. You are friendly but not clingy. When you arrive, spend time greeting everyone you see. Shake hands and smile.

Figure 4
Your author building rapport with a member of a participant's household.
Photo by Nelle Steele.

Thank them for offering you access to their home or office. Once you have greeted everyone you see, make sure you also greet pets. You may think I'm being a bit silly by making this point, but it's actually very important. If you are allergic, it will give you a moment to explain why you're not cuddling with Fluffy. If you are a genuine dog or cat lover, like I am, it will give you an ice-breaker moment to chat casually with your participants and put them at ease. Both pets and children provide an opportunity for the adult humans to drop their social pretenses and connect with each other. It will be a relaxing moment before you sit down.

Office or workplace ethnographies require a slightly different approach. You are still a guest in this private place, but at a workplace you are also expected to be unobtrusive. This is a place of business, whose primary activity is being productive. Workplace ethnographers often find themselves relegated to "out of the way" places in order to keep daily production humming. In her ethnography of computer chip manufacturing plants, Brigitte Jordan (2009) found herself often being given "tours" that were really designed to keep her out of the way. She noticed that there was a distinct "upstairs/downstairs" dynamic, wherein certain classes of workers worked on different floors, and her access differed depending on where she was. She found shyly asking for a cigarette with workers on their smoke breaks was an effective way of breaking the ice. She was no longer "on a tour" but simply hanging out with plant workers. She also tried another tack to get off the tour. As an external consultant, she found her access changed when she partnered with an internal researcher who was symbolically already part of the team. Between her efforts at hanging out and becoming more of an insider through her research partner, she discovered far more than she would have had she simply stayed "on the tour."

Depending on what you are there to find out, you may find yourself sitting down at the kitchen table or a conference room not long after you arrive. This may mean—in the immediate term—that you can only witness what your "handlers" want you to witness. This is where rapport building comes in. Your participant, whether he be the homeowner or the office manager, is the gatekeeper to your ethnographic experience. Allow him to be so. I recommend accepting any food or drink offered by the participant because it is a way for him to welcome you symbolically into his home or office. North Americans are often dismissive of this ritualistic welcome when they arrive somewhere "for business," but it is yet another opportunity for your participant to be at ease and make small talk. Accept that cup of coffee and have a chat while your participant prepares it. When he sits down opposite you, you should already have your notebook out. Your role is to make him feel comfortable and to trust you. This cannot be done if you demand access to the server room or the participant's bedroom.

The Beginning (Kind Of)

In this moment of sitting down, I'm often reminded of when I lived in Kiev in my early 20s. I was about to rent an apartment and had recruited my friend Yuriy to come with me to seal the deal. Though I spoke Russian, I figured the legality of the moment required a little more cultural know-how than I had. We arrived at the apartment and were ushered to the dining room table for tea. Suddenly, there was a ceremonious moment when my landlady, her daughter, and Yuriy all brought out their "passports," which were really what those of us in the West would call "your papers, please." Confused, I scrambled to find my Canadian passport and present it when everyone else presented theirs. I wondered if we were about to stamp each other's passports? No, it turns out, it was customary simply to show each other these papers, which confirmed you were a legal resident of the city. Once that moment had passed, everyone became more comfortable, and the business at hand commenced.

This moment marked "the beginning" of the meeting. Symbolically, this moment represented an exchange of trust. In the former Soviet Union, people were brought up to be wary of strangers, lest they report them to the authorities for some kind of violation. Showing one's papers is a ceremony of reciprocal transparency; both parties are rendered bare and vulnerable, and both parties are put at ease. After this moment, it was possible to continue. It was a moment both sides expected.

Participants in ethnography expect a "moment" as well, though many are not quite sure what that moment is. Unlike my former landlady, most participants have never been through "the beginning" of this kind of encounter. They may have a vague idea of what it entails, but they are looking to the ethnographer to signal the "beginning." Most participants will believe your research begins when you open your notebook and ask the first question. Seasoned ethnographers will know that you begin your research as you drive up to the home or office. Observations and all that small talk is relevant. But your participant will be expecting "the beginning" of the interview. You should not disappoint them.

The beginning is usually marked with the signing of the informed consent form. Participants generally want this moment to ceremoniously agree to the experience, and ethnographers usually like this moment to gather their thoughts before beginning the interview phase of the research. It will also give the participant a moment to gather *his* thoughts before you begin the conversation. Initiating this moment is just a touch of business-like flourish, but it will provide comfort to your participant; you do, in fact, have professional standards, and there is something "official" about this meeting. It is a moment that signals the encounter has officially begun, and the participant will appreciate it being marked ceremoniously.

A Year in the Field? Private-Sector Ethnography's Timelines

In this reflective book, *Tales from the Field,* ethnographer John Van Maanen explores the experience of ethnographic work, from a very personal perspective. In the 2010 "epilogue," Van Maanen laments once more the emotional costs ethnographers incur when they spend a year—or more—in the field. Yet, let us examine this claim more carefully. What would that year look like, for participants?

In her study of the collection of personal data, Abby Margolis (2013) sought to understand how and in what ways so-called "quantified self" technologies fit into a typical Western European or North American person's life. Imagine if she had spent the year in the field with participants. She might have visited them regularly, either at home or at work. The participant may have had long stretches of stressful overwork, especially if he or she was a highly paid professional. The participant would have celebrated holidays and birthdays, seen his or her child through a year of school, and perhaps lost or found a job. Margolis would have witnessed or learned about all of these significant milestones and rituals.

Would that have been necessary? Likely, a year would uncover simply too much data. Margolis learned five key misperceptions we collectively have about personal data, including the false conflation of personal data with "big data," and that personal data's value is in its sale. Margolis found that individuals used personal data for themselves only and did not aggregate it like big data. Additionally, participants found value in seeing and playing with their own data, not selling it to corporations. But if she had followed these participants for an entire year, they would likely have collected a lot of extraneous information that would have added only marginal improvements to their findings.

The typical private-sector project is focused on a single topic, so that observation over an entire year would actually get in the way of understanding the topic at hand. In the case of participants' experience of collecting and using their own personal data, following them for an entire year would have possibly uncovered interesting insights about year-end reflective rituals, or perhaps shown how personal data collection changes over time. But is the additional value of these insights worth delaying the project's completion for 12 months? Is it worth it for a product design team to wait an entire year before learning how personal data are used? Most private-sector ethnographers find that it isn't worth spending the entire 12 academic months in the field, and instead choose to focus on short, narrow studies on particular topics.

The Ethnographic Interview

In his wonderfully approachable book, *The Long Interview,* Grant McCracken (1988) notes that ethnography typically involves understanding culture, *writ large*. But private-sector ethnography can indeed study small slices of culture, within the confines of an extended, *in situ* interview. He points out that few social scientists have the time for full-blown ethnography, much less do *participants* have the time to allow social scientists into their lives for extended periods. But he maintains that with a cultural eye, the long interview can, in fact, offer ethnographic insight into specific topic areas. The secret, according to McCracken, is to focus on cultural aspects of your topic. In other words, focus on norms, practices, beliefs, and belief systems, and your "long interview" can provide ethnographic insight.

Many academic ethnographers spend at least a "season" or a year in the field with participants. This rough guideline is ostensibly so that an ethnographer may experience the full breadth of seasonal rituals and activities. But spending a year in the field is not only unnecessary, it may even be counter-productive.

Spradley (1979) details the key aspects of this kind of fieldwork in his book, *The Ethnographic Interview*. He argues that this kind of interview is more akin to a "friendly conversation" than a traditional interview. This means that establishing rapport with participants and allowing the conversation to flow naturally are key elements. But ethnographers must go further than just being good conversationalists; they must also target the conversation around a particular topic area, and they must focus on ethnographic aspects of the topic. This means that, in practice, the ethnographic interview appears to be a naturally flowing conversation, which just so happens to focus mostly on norms, practices, and beliefs.

The interview is perhaps the easiest part of private-sector ethnography because participants are generally familiar with the concept. Sitting at that kitchen table, or in that conference room, your job is to methodically go through the topic areas sketched out in your interview guide. You will find your participant taking tangents (or, if he's anything like the young people I've interviewed lately, taking phone calls and texts in the middle of the interview!). You must bring the focus of the conversation back consistently to the general topic at hand, and probe carefully around the socio-cultural aspects of that topic. Now you will notice why "reading around" is so important. Having a theoretical orientation before you go into the field will allow you to bring the conversation back to a general social concept, such as gender roles, cultural capital, or the presentation of self.

The Tour

Depending on your topic area, you will mostly likely need to see some physical aspect of your participants' environments. For example, I did for an engineering company which was moving from 2D design software to

3D design software. I spent time sitting in a conference room with engineers and designers, and then I asked to see their workstations. I was doing more than simply getting a sense of what their environment was like; I was gathering important data about the tools they used on a daily basis.

The tour of the home or office can take place at any point during the field visit, but I usually find it's a good ice breaker to conduct it near the beginning. It allows the ethnographer to gain access to the entire location of study. Having a tour is a symbolic introduction of the ethnographer to the location, which is, after all, also a subject of the study. The tour will allow the ethnographer to get introduced to more people that work or live there, and will provide her with some familiarity of the layout of the environment. A tour is also a primary moment of data collection. Understanding the symbolic arrangement of the environment provides clues to the domestic or workplace culture. For example, in one study I conducted on smartphone use at work and home (Ladner, 2012), I toured participants' homes as a way of learning where technology is "allowed" to be located. I found that the bedroom often had few if any technologies. I also learned that smartphones often had close-at-hand spaces reserved for them in participants' cars and office desks. Some participants even had a space for smartphones in the front hall, symbolically communicating that the phone was "unwelcome" in the rest of the home, and must stay in the hall, away from the family.

The tour is a very important portion of fieldwork. If you do not gain access to the participants' environment, you have a very limited view of their aesthetic preferences and domestic or office technology ecosystems. It is during the tour that you will learn what kinds of tools your participants are already using, which is critical to building a product that fits into these people's lives. It is during the tour that you'll learn that their lives are orderly, or chaotic, or sad. It is during the tour that you'll find evidence that belies their contentions that they "only ever use Apple products," or that they cook with their oven four to five times a week. Gaps between what they tell you and what they actually do come alive during the tour.

It is during this time that you may ask permission to take still photographs of artifacts or items of interest. You may be an excellent note taker and might be able to document all the objects that are relevant to your study. But it's unlikely that lists of words will have much impact on your clients and stakeholders. "A picture is worth a thousand words" is more than just a saying. A few snapshots of your participants' environments will convey a great deal of information to your clients quickly. They will also help you in your analysis because it will be a rich data set from which you can draw repeatedly as you sift through your interview notes. When I take still photos in participants' environments, I usually turn the flash to "off" and the shutter sound to "silent" so that I may quickly snap photographs without disturbing the natural flow of the conversation. I never take covert photographs, however, because it is the participant's right to be informed and actively consent to all aspects of the interview.

Sometimes a tour is not possible. I had one participant who refused to show us his home computer, which was in the bedroom that was "too messy." Even though the recruiters had clearly articulated this to be a condition of participation, I had to respect the participant's wishes. It was his home and his right to refuse any part of the interview. As a sociologist, it is my ethical duty to put the participant in the driver's seat and determine what parts of the experience he will participate in. It was also his home; it was my duty as a guest to respect my host's wishes. If you are refused access to parts of the environment, this is the category of the "known unknowns." In the case of my participant who refused me entry to his bedroom, I used my smartphone to ask him to mimic his online searching method, which is what we were interested in. Was this ideal? Not at all. Was it ethical? Yes, absolutely.

The Observation

What do people want in an office chair? If you ask them, they will tell you they want lots of cushioning, for comfort. Ethnographic techniques discovered that what people say they want contrasts directly with what they actually need. Before they designed their famous Aeron Chair, Bill Stumpf and Don Chadwick began their design process with observation. They visited dozens of offices and observed real people sitting in their chairs. What they discovered was that, over time, office workers would begin to squirm, not because they were uncomfortable, but because their chairs were hot. This led them to the famous weave design of the Aeron chair, which allows for maximum airflow (Martin, 2009). Eventually, the chair was "tested"

Becoming a "Cold Ethnographer": How to Hide in Plain Sight

1. Budget sufficient time: There is nothing more forced, more contrived than an ethnographer arriving and expecting an immediate display of "normal" behavior. Normal behavior does occur in every potential research site, but it takes time for it to resume. Budget time for this settling down process to happen. Do not force your participants to "act natural" immediately upon your arrival. Give them the opportunity to mark the novelty of your arrival. Eventually, they will need to return to their normal activities.

2. Be quiet: People who are comfortable interviewing people are often uncomfortable with total silence. Cultivate your inner introvert by intentionally not saying anything. After arriving at the site and introducing yourself and perhaps taking a tour or having a sit-down interview, practice sitting silently. Absolutely, explain to participants that this is part of the research process, but work consciously to say nothing.

3. Hands-in-pockets: Nothing is more intimidating than a researcher with a notebook or microphone. The moment you place your hands in your pockets, the research experience is transformed. Participants now feel that you are no longer watching them and that they can return to their regular lives. The challenge with placing your hands in your pockets is that you cannot take notes. This is where true ethnographic skills arise; good ethnographers have good memories and discipline about field notes.

4. Practice disruption: One way to get better at ethnographic observation is to practice it in your everyday life. When you go to a movie theatre, ask the attendant a question about the building. See what happens. When you are shopping for shoes, ask fellow shoppers what drives them to try on a pair. Get comfortable with the disruption it causes. After you intentionally cause a social disruption, practice the tips above: take your time, be silent, or put your hands in pockets. Learn what works for you.

with focus groups, who widely pronounced the chair ugly and "unfinished." Yet it went on to be one of the best-selling office chairs of all time, and came to symbolize the new spirit of the dot-com era.

It was observation, plus a little courage, that allowed Stumpf and Chadwick to stay true to their design vision. Observation is of the most important and underrated aspect of field work. Interviewing is very important to find out what participants are thinking, but observation offers that key ethnographic differentiator: the gap between what participants say and what they do. Observation requires the careful noticing of what is happening, how and with what tools it is happening, and perhaps most interesting, what is not happening. People were not fetching extra pillows and placing them on their office chairs, as Stumpf and Chadwick watched. They were squirming but not seeking extra padding.

Observation creates what my friend and ethnographic filmmaker Bruno Moynié calls "the hot camera." When Moynié arrives at the site with his camera, he finds that participants tend to focus directly on the camera and its presence. The camera is "hot" in that it attracts attention and makes participants a little nervous. But over time, and after significant work building rapport with participants, the camera becomes "cold" in that participants forget about its presence and begin to return to their natural way of being. Whether with a camera or not, there is such a thing as a "hot ethnographer" problem. The ethnographer's presence is noticeable, disruptive, and genuinely alters the experience of everyday life in that location. Becoming a "cold ethnographer" can happen with a few techniques.

Observation is much easier to effect in large, busy places where the ethnographer can fade into the background. I have found in my own experience that it's easier to blend into workplaces than into homes. Ethnographer Thomas Malaby eventually blended into Linden Labs, the makers of the virtual world Second Life. Malaby got invited to team meetings and sat on the edge of discussions while people got on with the business of development. Malaby noticed that the developers imprinted their ideals of competition and the free market onto the algorithms that governed Second Life, even though they overtly said that competition was not something they set out to engineer specifically (Malaby, 2009).

Leaving

Ethnographic interviews usually last between two and three hours. Sometimes participants lose track of time and will happily chat with you for four hours. But typically, you will exhaust all of your focused, topical questions after about two hours. The tour may be a more involved affair, such as one that involves you participating in or observing a specific task, like using an existing file management system on an office computer or baking a cake in a home kitchen. Given that most private-sector ethnography mirrors McCraken's concept of the focused "long interview," this amount of time is sufficient to learn about a participant and her world. Multiply this by 10 or 15 participants, and you have upwards of 30 to 45 hours of observation and interviewing. That is a fantastically huge data set, which, unlike focus groups, also includes contextual artifacts.

It is often quite apparent when it's time to leave a participant's home or office. Usually, the topic focus that private-sector ethnography demands is exhausted by the two hour mark (the ethnographer and the participant are often exhausted by this point, too!). At this point, when it is obvious your time together has run its course, it is up to you to end the interview. Participants will not be rude (generally) and are unlikely to ask you to leave. So it is up to you, as the astute guest, to signal it's time to leave. I usually end the interview with another ceremonious event: the presentation of the incentive, if you have one. I often also like to ask if I might contact them in the future should we have any further questions. This often does happen, and it's good to ask for this question when you've established a rapport.

At this point, participants are usually relieved and even a bit puzzled at how enjoyable the experience was. I had one physician whom I interviewed in his office. I and my colleague spent three hours in his office, chatting with him and his secretary, and "hanging out" while he would see patients. By lunch time, he was genuinely sad to see us leave. He expressed surprise at his own feelings, saying that it had been the most enjoyable contact he'd ever had with market researchers. He noted he'd participated in focus groups in the past and always found them too focused on tiny details and not interested in his role as a physician. The way he put it was that in focus groups, they might ask you "Which hat do you like best?" and he might want to say, "But I don't need a hat; I need an elephant!" In the ethnographic interview, he felt he could explain why he might need an elephant, and that his experience might finally be understood. My colleague and I took this as a huge compliment (some high-fiving may have followed).

Immediately following a field visit, you should spend at least 20 minutes summarizing your immediate first impressions. I usually do this by sitting in my car, and quickly writing up my notes, focusing on the key areas of interest. These 20 minutes are the extremely valuable, as the experience is still fresh in your mind. You'll remember more in those 20 minutes than you will even 20 hours later, so take the time to write down your thoughts and observations. You will thank yourself as the number of interviews increases and all the data swim in your head.

An Example

Let me explain how a field visit might play out using an example. Returning to our example of young men and video games, the ethnographer may find that she doesn't have the time to spend a full month or two, hanging out with her participant and his roommates. But she still wants to understand the cultural aspects of video game playing and to develop a holistic view of her participants' video game experience. She will use these data to help her design team make more compelling story lines, or to help her marketing team develop a more authentic and meaningful voice.

The ethnographer may have a working theory or hunch that masculinity, coming-of-age, and autonomy are related to video game playing for young men. So in her visit, she may pay attention to areas of shared space versus personal space, and how video game playing fits into that. She may take about 10 still photographs of shared and personal spaces. She may take another five of objects that signify this coming-of-age struggle, particularly those that embody masculine traits and those that are dear to the participant. She may record over 90 minutes of audio as she interviews the participant about his video game playing, and record another 15 pages of field notes during the tour.

Many private-sector and academic ethnographers mistake time in the field as an indicator of fieldwork quality. In reality, it is the analysis of that time in the field that is the most important. Certainly, you can learn more about a person and his world if you spend more time there with him. But no amount of time with him will substitute for a lack of insight into social life in general. Again, this is why theory is so important to fieldwork.

Understanding the role of theory is part of the process of "Oh my god, I'm doing ethnography" jitters. But after six or seven projects, you should have just "regular fieldwork" jitters. Fieldwork is indeed a difficult skill to master, but even the most experienced interviewers and observers will face a challenge if they return from the field with no strategy on how to analyze their data. Theoretical constructs help reduce our data into manageable chunks, as you will see in the next chapter.

Chapter 9
Analysis

It is just before September 11, 2001. I am standing in my sunny apartment on 12th Avenue in Vancouver.[1] I am writing my master's thesis. It is my first foray into ethnography. I had interviewed participants and spent a month in Toronto, doing observational fieldwork. Now back in Vancouver, and the excitement of fieldwork over, I am lost. My field notes, scrawled into (paper!) notebooks, lie scattered across my desk. My desktop computer, with its enormous CRT monitor, holds all my audio recordings. There is a blanket of Post-it notes on my apartment wall. I see myself, staring at that wall, arms crossed and brow wrinkled. I have no idea what I'm doing.

At the end of fieldwork, you will most likely find yourself, like Malinowski and me, floating in your own "chaotic mess of notes." That is absolutely normal and completely expected. I remember reading Creswell's (1994) advice to use "axial coding," but I did not know what that meant. Did it refer to the axes of a chart? To car axles? What was he trying to tell me? How do you actually analyze qualitative data?

I want to tell my neophyte self (and any neophytes reading this book) that qualitative data analysis can be very straightforward. Just like quantitative social researchers, ethnographers must do two things: describe the data and interpret the data. Description of ethnographic data requires summarization. Quantitative researchers have it a bit

Practical Ethnography: A Guide to Doing Ethnography in the Private Sector by Sam Ladner, 139–157. © 2014 Left Coast Press, Inc. All rights reserved.

easier; they can summarize data with the very straightforward measures of central tendency and dispersion. Mean scores and standard deviations sum up quantitative data with the push of a computer keyboard button. Ethnographers don't have it as easy, but they can describe the same kind of thing, just without numbers: what is common and what is divergent about your participants? Interpretation is more difficult. Quantitative researchers seek to offer prediction, through cross-tabulation, tests of significance, correlations, regression analysis, and analysis of variance. Qualitative researchers, remember, cannot make predictive claims. So instead we must answer what our chosen topic means for *these particular participants*.

Qualitative data analysis is difficult. Many novice researchers only offer description and fail to offer interpretation because they have so little social theory to guide them. It is theory, not method, that differentiates good research from poor research. It is theory that guides the ethnographer through his chaotic mess of notes. Even the most ruthlessly reductionist ethnographers often find themselves shocked at the sheer volume of information they end up with at the end of their fieldwork phase. This information overload is deeply ironic, of course, since we ethnographers expend huge amounts of energy defending our so-called small sample size.

You might have already noticed, by this point, how many times I've discussed data reduction throughout this book. When you design your research question, you are narrowing your focus to a topic that will produce actionable, specific results. When you recruit, you are zeroing in on a particular type of person, and leaving out just "people" in general. When you interview, you are bringing participants back to the topic at hand in order to minimize the amount of data you must sort through. All along the ethnographic project, you are reducing, reducing, reducing. By the time you reach the analysis phase, you should have set yourself up for a relatively straightforward process of answering your research questions by further reducing your data, summarizing it, and interpreting it.

This chapter is about how to make sense of your data. If you took a short-cut directly to this chapter, hoping to analyze the data you now have scattered throughout notebooks and computer hard drives, you will likely be disappointed. First and foremost, you will have missed the tips for reducing your data that are liberally sprinkled throughout this book.

Secondly, and most importantly, you will have no theoretical frame to help you separate the important from the merely interesting. If you have no grounding in theory, you will not be able to tell your clients and stakeholders what your participants' experiences mean. That is the critical jump from description to interpretation.

Questions Ethnographers Do Not Answer

Private-sector social research faces an essential challenge: business people tend to focus on questions about their products, rather than questions about *people*. Ethnographers do not study products; they study how products fit (or do not fit) into people's lives. In other words, ethnographers answer questions about people, while business people expect answers about products. This gap often makes analysis difficult. Managing expectations about what you will and will not answer in your final report is key to gaining the trust and repeat business of your clients.

Private-sector clients may expect answers about their product's competitive standing in participants' minds: How do we stack up to the competition? Clients may expect to learn about product performance or quality: How does our product compare in terms of quality? Clients may expect to learn how well their product might sell: How likely are customers to buy our product? They may even expect to learn *from participants* how to innovate: What do customers think we should we do to improve our product? Ethnography will not reliably answer these questions. Robust competitive analysis is best done through comprehensive surveys with large sample sizes. Ethnography may uncover some illustrative details about the competition, but it will not provide a stacked ranking of your client's products. It most certainly will not provide any predictions about future sales. It may provide some insight into potential areas for innovation, but it is not a *customer's* job to innovate products; that is the product manager or designer's job. Ethnography will uncover potential areas for improvement or unmet needs, but it will not answer the questions, "How many consumers prefer our competitor's product?" or "What exact product should we build to beat the competition?"

The ethnographic enterprise is to understand people, their beliefs, attitudes, norms, and behaviors. Your role as the data analyst is to make the connections between what participants do and say, and what your stakeholders want to know about their products. The connections will not be immediately obvious, but this is precisely why private-sector ethnography is highly skilled work.

To Transcribe or Not to Transcribe?

Academic ethnographers almost always transcribe their interview recordings. Not only do they typically have the time to do so, they are also expected to deeply analyze the text of each interview with a high degree of rigor. The text of participants' words is the primary focus in this kind of analysis. This has limitations, of course. How and in what way participants talk is left out in a textual analysis. It also has advantages. Analysis of text allows the ethnographer to write up her findings in article or book format, which is exactly the kind of reporting expected in academia.

Private-sector ethnographers rarely have either the time or the need to transcribe entire interviews. They don't often produce articles or books about their findings, and the ways in which participants express themselves are actually very important. It is also quite possible to gain sufficient insight from ethnographic data without transcribing interviews if—and this is a big if—the ethnographer has taken good field notes and written thoughtful analytic memos throughout fieldwork.

Direct quotes are still very important, so it's important to spend the time to accurately reflect what your participants have said. Often, researchers turn to transcription when they take poor field notes. This is a fool's errand. Knowing what is significant has more to do with having enough "with-it-ness" in the field than in having enough time to examine the interview transcripts. Having transcripts will not give you magical powers of insight, though they do give you more time to consider and reflect. Chances are that if you believe transcribing interviews will uncover substantially new insights, the problem is that you didn't know what was important before you went into the field. Again, this is where theory comes in.

But there are contemporary tools to help you take note of significant statements while in the field. The solution lies in "bookmarking" important parts of the interview as you are conducting it. This can be done several ways. I tend to bookmark using my Livescribe pen. When a participant says something of interest, you can either make a note saying that in your notebook, or you can simply hit the star or "favorites" button at the bottom of the notebook. Granted, even the best ethnographers will hit the favorites button only *after* the participant has said the magic words, so you must backtrack slightly when listening to the audio. Livescribe has a function to allow you to do exactly that as you listen to the playback, so that you zero in only on the most important parts, and transcribe those accurately. Another option is using tools built for radio journalists, which have similar bookmarking functionality. I have used Hindenburg, the iPhone app and its desktop radio mixing tool. When in the field, the Hindenburg app allows you to record your interviews digitally. When a participant says something important, you can inconspicuously tap the app, and it will bookmark that moment in the audio recording. Unfortunately, I have yet to find this type of functionality in any video recording tool.

The Process of Analyzing Ethnographic Data

In their valuable book, *Qualitative Data Analysis*, Miles and Huberman (1994) offer a very straightforward set of steps for any kind of qualitative data analysis:

1. Reduce
2. Visualize
3. Draw conclusions and verify

Data reduction should be relatively easy if you have been reducing your data all along through the project. I like to say that you "prune" your data, because you tend to it as it grows. You may notice, for example, halfway through your fieldwork that you are gathering a set of photographs that may be just outside your preferred topic area. You wonder if they will become relevant. You decide to "prune" them by putting them aside in another folder so that you may focus on only the most relevant photos now. Your data are still growing, but in a much more focused way. But even with such pruning, by the analysis phase, chances are you need to reduce your data even further.

Reduction Techniques

The first step in analysis for private-sector ethnographers is simply to describe what they heard and observed in the field. This step, in the broadest of senses, is about summarization, which is the most common reduction method. Describing quantitative data through summarization is really much easier. Concepts like "average" are deeply familiar to most people working in the private sector, making quick summaries possible and understandable. How do you summarize qualitative data?

Paraphrasing

The simplest way to summarize is to paraphrase what your participants said about key topics. You do not need, nor can you possibly use, direct quotes from each participant on each key topic. The art of paraphrasing is about capturing the main idea your participant conveyed, but to make it much more succinct and even a little more interesting. For example, this is one of my participants, describing why he and his company chose to purchase Apple computers:

> Our product is being developed on a Mac. It means that the Mac is going to be a part of our product. We are selling a system that includes a computer which is a Mac. Because of the information and human resources we had at the time when we had to make a decision, the Mac seemed to be the quickest platform to develop on and had the most integrated product in terms of the GUI, etc. Based on the experts that were actually doing the work, apparently developing on OSX is really easy and good. Apple also has that integrated hardware/software thing going on…because they have that high level of control, it extends to software development.

How can you paraphrase this quote effectively? Pull out the important ideas this participant is trying to convey. First, the participant is explaining the context in which the decision was made. Specifically, they had time pressures to get the product developed as quickly as possible. He also explains that their employees at the time had a skill set that matched the Mac platform. Secondly, he mentions that he was influenced by "experts" (which we later learned he found through forums like Github. com and Stackoverflow.com). Finally, he also mentions that the hardware

Table 5: Examples of Good Direct Quotes

Quote	Context	Why it's interesting
"Some things need to be top-down but I think we over-did it."	CEO describing how they might have lost their creative spirit	Describes a senior manager's perception on innovation and his organization's failings
"It's kind of a panicky thing. I thought, oh my god, what if I have lung cancer?"	Asthma patient describes what's it's like to get a diagnosis	Evokes emotional response
"I started watching Fashion Television when I was five."	Mom of two describes how important fashion is to her	Irreverent response provides character detail
"The days of the doctor being a god is way gone. Patients' families are demanding. It's a demanding society. They demand service. "	Physician describing the change in patient-physician interaction and power	Quickly summarizes many decades' worth of change in a single profession

and software integration of Apple allowed them to make a simple and tightly controlled development environment. This participant's quote could be paraphrased like this:

> Andre's decision to purchase Mac computers stemmed from the easy-to-use development platform, which was compatible with their existing skills and was recommended by leading developers.

This paraphrase can be stitched together with other paraphrases and suddenly you have a working theory for why startup founders might purchase Apple computers. Take the time to paraphrase all but the most important, compelling, and uniquely phrased direct quotes. Most of what your participants say can be paraphrased.

Many novice ethnographers struggle trying to discern when something is interesting and when something should be a direct quote. A direct quote worth repeating typically offers a colorful, character-revealing statement, or the precise phrase you want your clients and stakeholders to hear. The participant either paints a picture about himself in a unique way, or he perfectly summarizes a key insight you want your stakeholders to hear. See Table 5 for a selection of direct quotes from some of my research.

Participant Data Cards

You can quickly reduce down your two to three hour field visits into a single data card. After each visit, make a separate document that is intentionally short. It should summarize the participant's demographic details, a single quote that epitomizes her take on the world, and how her experience answers your original research questions. Students of design will see how the data card could easily translate into a design persona.

The card can take many forms, but I still enjoy doing it the old-fashioned way: on actual index cards. The index card's small size forces brevity, and the act of copying it out by hand imprints the participant on my brain. I don't stop there, however. I use Evernote to take a picture of the data card, and Evernote's built-in handwriting recognition makes the data card searchable.

The Cohering Metaphor

Metaphors are a fundamental way we humans organize and understand our world. (Lakoff and Johnson, 1999), yet researchers rarely use them to summarize their findings. Metaphors are perhaps the best way to quickly summarize complex ideas and nuanced findings of qualitative research. Generating a powerful and effective metaphor is simpler than it appears. I return to Denny and Sunderland's very simple question: "What is x?" In their example, they ask, "What is coffee?" One answer they offer is that coffee is a way to soften the awkwardness of new business relationships. "Coffee as business lubricant" could be a simple metaphor to summarize this finding. This kind of answer can cohere a marketing strategy, a design for a new café, an advertising campaign, or a packaging design. It will allow you to focus your end product around the cultural meaning of the phenomenon you are studying. When you ask "What is x?" you are developing a cohering metaphor that encapsulates the holistic, cultural, and symbolic meaning of the phenomenon you are studying.

This works for both marketing concepts and user experience concepts. I once worked on developing an online product selection tool. In the course of this design process, my team asked, "What is this 'online selection tool'?" I described the tool as "hop on, hop off," meaning that the user decides where he "hops on" the selection tool to learn about and compare products. When he has learned enough, he "hops off" the selection tool and begins the purchasing process. Most people were familiar with this concept of the "hop on, hop off" tourist bus, which allows tourists to choose how much or how little of the city they see. The selection tool was designed to allow online shoppers to choose how much or how little product information they see before they decide to make a purchase. Consider another example. If you are studying how dads influence purchasing decisions of cleaning supplies, you are answering, "What is a 'cleaning product' for dads?" Perhaps you find that by purchasing cleaning supplies, dads are substituting domestic labor for household provisioning. Maybe they aren't actually doing the cleaning, but they are still supporting the endeavor. Your metaphor could be "cleaning supplies as household redemption." An ethnographer's job is to provide a holistic answer to such questions, which in turn provides a cohering metaphor or explanatory framework of this particular phenomenon.

Describing Behaviors

In addition to the cohering metaphor, ethnographers can turn to social theory to help reduce and summarize their data. Using some simple and quite old social theories will help you here.[2] Glaser and Strauss (1967) offer a very straightforward framework for analysis. Your job is to summarize:

1. Interactions among actors
2. Conditions of these interactions
3. Strategies and tactics actors employ
4. Consequences

This framework is particularly useful for design research projects, which often focus on usability failures. I find it particularly enlightening to document all the strategies and tactics actors employ to deal with a system's usability failures. Human-computer interaction experts often call these strategies "workarounds." At times, they become elaborate detours that users may not even realize they have crafted for themselves. Documenting and summarizing the strategies and tactics gives your design partners specific directions for what to correct in the systems.

Simply by describing participants' behavior, ethnographers can uncover clues that can help designers create better solutions. For example, in their ethnography of paper mail inside the home, Richard Harper and Brian Shatwell (2003) found some clear advantages paper has over email, simply by describing what they admitted appeared to be a mundane behavior. Women in their study tended to pick up paper mail from the front hall and put the paper in places where the men might see it. One woman, for example, put an electric bill in a physically prominent location so that her male partner might see it and pay the bill. After several days, the bill was still there, so she paid it herself. This mundane domestic experience actually revealed a great deal about gender roles and what Harper and Shatwell call "workflow affordances" of paper. Women manage men, and paper's very design allows for it to construct a workflow, simply by being put in a specific location (they note that email lacks this affordance in its design).

In fieldwork, you may discover that not all members of a particular office use the "official" system to get their work done. Yet there are still many other members of that office that do use that system. How do you describe these contradictory behaviors? Remember, of course, that Malinowksi noted that actors flout the rules almost as much as they follow them. Another framework to summarize all kinds of behaviors is Linton's (1936) theory. Linton argues that every culture has a sanctioned set of behaviors. Whether it is the island of Samoa or an office of engineers, groups of people develop a definition of what normal is, and members may or may not "follow the rules." There are:

1. Universals: what everyone does or should do. I like to use the example of shoes. Everyone should wear shoes.

2. Specialties: what do some members of the group do? This often tells you something about power or perhaps gender roles. In the case of shoes, *women* wear high heels, thus demonstrating their "special" role as enacting femininity through body adornment.

3. Alternatives: these behaviors are within the realm of "personal taste," but are often considered unusual. Members will tolerate this behavior but may find it a little eccentric. For example, wearing bright pink Doc Martens might be an alternative behavior.

4. Peculiarities: what is outside the realm of acceptable behavior. These go beyond personal taste into behaviors that would be actively discouraged through outright sanction or more subtle ostracism. For example, not wearing any shoes at all may invite sanctions such as "No shirt, no shoes, no service."

Visualization Techniques

Once you have reduced your data to something manageable, you can see its significance by visualizing it. Miles and Huberman's list of visual displays provides options for diagramming everyday business ideas. These displays (see Table 6) are optimized for academic studies, not private sector ones, so their language and parlance must be slightly adapted to fit the applied setting. For example, Miles and Huberman suggest that a "time-ordered display" can show how a process works or does not work. This translates well into the idea of the "customer journey," which is a common way to describe the entire experience of purchasing a product or service. Private-sector clients often do not see the entire customer journey because, as Gibbs (1998) explains, they often have a very narrow view of what he calls the "consumption act." The consumption act goes beyond the single moment when a consumer purchases a product, yet many of your clients may not consider the entire purchasing experience. It includes the time when the consumer is made aware of a product, when she is actively considering a product and weighing her options, as well as the moment of purchase and the experience after purchase. Many in the private sector call this last phase the "unboxing" or the "out of the box" experience. It is something that Apple has mastered, with its beautifully designed product boxes that rival the products themselves in simplicity and ease of use. Diagramming the "customer journey" (aka the "time-ordered display") provides a quick way of showing your clients the consumption act and where it might be unpleasant for consumers.

I used a time-ordered display in my project on Christmas lights. My role was to add depth and context to the customer journey, with an eye to uncovering pain points and potential design solutions. If you've ever put up Christmas lights, you will know that there is indeed a lot of pain involved! My ethnography revealed all the steps the customer took to put up Christmas lights.

Table 6: Time-Ordered Display of the Christmas Lights Customer Journey

Stage	Name
Stage 0	Inventory
	Participants "check" their lights and ensure that they have all the basic supplies to complete the job. They are re-familiarizing themselves with the items they need to put up the lights. This requires actually *looking* at the items. There is a pulling out and opening of boxes. This is a half-hearted poke around. In fact, many of our participants were doing this inventory for this project. There is little urgency about the process.
Stage 1	Christmas Thinking
	Participants are picking up general signals about the coming Christmas season. The signals are in stores, magazines, on television, on the radio, and in their workplaces. It is also sometimes through their children's experiences at school. This phase happens only after Halloween is over. Participants at this stage are "dreaming" of Christmas, musing about Christmas in general. There is little concrete planning. It involves creating a mental mood board of the look and feel of this year's decorations.
Stage 2	Purchase and Prep
	Participants in this stage are getting into project management mode. The goal here is to gather all the materials necessary for the outdoor lighting and the indoor decorations. This is a concerted process with specific goals and some urgency. It involves verifying the mental list of requirements generated in Stage 0. It also involves The Drive to the Store, which may actually be several drives to several stores. Specificity is now required.
Stage 3	Decorate
	Participants are now in execution mode. This day (or days) is usually the "first nice day" that occurs after Christmas Thinking. It may be the same day as Stage 2 (which makes for a very long day). Participants on this day have very specific goals that must be completed by the end of the day. The end of this day is quite satisfying and often involves a self-congratulatory drink.
Stage 4:	Top-up Trip
	Participants in this optional stage have been forced to get more supplies. Driving to the store after decoration has begun is particularly vexing. They will return to finish Stage 3. This stage is thankless, frustrating, and must be done quickly.

Stage	Name
Stage 5:	Experience
	Participants are managing the new lighting during this stage. This involves the turning off and on of lights (or outsourcing this responsibility to a timer if they have one). It also involves the enjoyment of the lights as the participants themselves pull into the driveway.
Stage 6:	Cancelling Christmas
	Participants in this stage are switching into archiving mode. Putting away decorations is often exhausting and even bittersweet. As a result, they may not employ good archiving practices. Everything, including the lights, goes away at this time. Participants may arbitrarily define some items as "winter-y" in order to keep them out on display. They may also make justifications for keeping "Christmas" lights up, including: they're "all year round lights" or "we just won't turn them on." Participants in this stage need help archiving items, and reasons to keep lights up.
Stage 6A	January Sales
	Few participants engage in this stage. This is the "Martha" character who seeks out sales in order to save money. She is already organized, so she needs little project management assistance. Participants in this stage are price motivated, but will not buy just anything.

Miles and Huberman offer quite a few more visualization techniques, including the "conceptually clustered matrix," which helps ethnographers describe high-level themes, and the "event-state network diagram," which shows the root causes of where problems occur. See all of these techniques, adapted from Miles and Huberman, in Table 7.

The "conceptually clustered matrix," for example, is a table that summarizes how participants interacted with or answered questions about particular products. It is a very quick way to summarize your participants' opinions. The "time-ordered matrix," by contrast, is a quick way to summarize a customer's journey through a particular product lifecycle. This type of display is particularly helpful for anything relating to user experience or the new customer acquisition process.

Table 7: Types of Qualitative Data Displays

	Display Name	Type	Description	Good for
Partially ordered	Context chart	Network style	Shows inter-relationships among roles and groups	Organizational research
	Checklist matrix	Table style	List of effects around a single variable	Deep understanding of one variable
Time ordered	Event listing	Table style	List of events or process	Understanding a process
	Critical incident chart	Table style	List of only key events over time	Understanding inflection points
	Event state network	Network style	Completed after event listing; shows context	Understanding causes and contexts of chronology
	Activity record	Network style	A narrative of each event in a detailed process, in node display	Showing details of multi-step process
	Decision modeling	Network style	Flow chart of events	Interactive flows and/or wireframes for web sites
	Time ordered matrix	Table style	A table, with time events as columns	Tracking key drivers of change
Role ordered	Role ordered matrix	Table style	Table summarizing roles in rows and variables in columns	In-depth understanding of single sites and roles within them
	Role-by-time matrix	Table style	A role-order matrix, with time as an additional column	Showing who does what when

	Display Name	Type	Description	Good for
Conceptually ordered	Conceptually clustered matrix	Table style	Table with participants in rows and research questions in columns	Answering original research questions, discerning patterns
	Thematic conceptual matrix	Table style	Table with themes in rows and variables in columns	Answering original research questions, setting up for quant
	Folk Taxonomy	Network style	Unstructured network diagram similar to a mental model, includes hierarchical ordering	Brain-storming causality
	Cognitive map	Network style	Unstructured diagram summarizing an individual's understanding of a phenomenon	Starting an aggregate mental model
	Effects matrix	Table style	A table for describing outcomes of particular events	Revealing what might be a dependent variable in future quant study

Drawing Conclusions

If description answers the question, "What happened?" interpretation can answer the question, "Why?" Ethnographic data contain insight into how customers think about a particular product. When coupled with social theory, ethnography can also provide an interpretation of what that product *actually means* to its customers. In short, you can explain why a customer chose a competitor, why she decided to stop buying more of the same brand, or perhaps why she won't recommend the product to someone else. This sort of interpretation cannot happen without some intellectual courage on the part of the ethnographer; he must take his summary and say, "This is what this means." It's an extraordinarily difficult and courageous thing to do.

Looking for Contradictions

Contradiction is an extremely useful opportunity to draw conclusions. Let's take an example. Suppose you are researching note-taking behaviors among college students. Your aim is to improve an existing web tool. You start by summarizing your findings, perhaps by generating a conceptually clustered matrix. You document the ways participants describe their note-taking tool, and then how they used the tool while you observed. Imagine that some of your participants claim to take careful notes in all of their classes. Yet during your observations, you notice that some of your participants take few if any notes at all. This kind of a contradiction often confuses and concerns novice ethnographers, but it really ought to excite them. This is precisely where deep insight will be found. So they *say* they take careful notes, but in practice, they don't. What does this imply for the note-taking tool? That it is a comforting signifier of one's own productivity, whether it is used or not. This means that its features, functionality, and go-to market strategy must cohere around the idea of the tool as "productivity performance" or a way to manage impressions of self. Contrary to first appearance, *actual* note-taking behavior is not the essence of the tool. It is the *idea* of note-taking behavior that is the essence of the tool.

The gap between what people say and what they do is a rich ground for finding contradictions. Another place to spot them is to ask participants what the "perfect" note-taker might do, and to compare that to what they themselves do. Often participants have a very clear opinion of what they themselves "should" be doing but, for whatever reason, are not doing. This reveals where a "universal" behavior begins and ends. Spotting contradiction is a first step toward explaining the true nature of a phenomenon.

Reversals

In his powerhouse of a book, *The Sociological Imagination,* sociologist C. Wright Mills advised novice sociologists to perform thought experiments using the idea of "reversal." Mills suggested that sociologists intentionally reverse the conditions they observe in order to understand the essence of the social phenomenon. If you are trying to understand despair, he writes, start by trying to understand elation. He notes that the act of contrasting extremes allows you to understand a concept better. If you're trying to understand the experience of flying commercial, think through the experience of flying on private jets. This thought experiment will reveal aspects like a lack of queues, easy access to the actual plane, dignity of person, and premium seating. Back to our note-taking study: you may have found that participants talk about the gap between their digital note-taking behavior and their professors' analogue behavior. A reversal question might be, "What is the nature of the professor's analogue note taking?" In this thought experiment, you may find yourself musing about the professor's "files" in his office, the physical co-location of his books and his personal notes. This may help you make an analogy to the note-taking tool's missing feature: personal notes connecting to *experts' notes.*

Reversals are especially fruitful when you are considering categories of race, class, or gender. In a study on men's preferences in interior design, ask yourself what a "woman cave" might look like. In a study on luxury goods, ask yourself what "luxury mayonnaise" or "luxury deodorant" might look like.

Explaining Outliers

Quantitative researchers really have it easy sometimes. When they find a data point (which represents a person, by the way) that does not fit the general pattern, they can label it an outlier and disregard its presence. Back when I did research on technology, innovation, and economic growth, my favorite outlier was Luxembourg. The country is so small that its per capita income is always at the top of the world list. But we know this is an outlier, so we typically exclude Luxembourg.

Qualitative researchers actually use outliers as a tool to understand everyone else that does fit the pattern. In her ethnography of work and family life, Arlie Hochschild (1997) met a man who was far more committed to childcare work than the other men she met. This man was the primary caregiver to his children and was always the one who picked them up from school. Unlike the other men in her study, this man appeared to have no ambivalence about being the caregiver. Other men grappled with feelings of emasculation, but this man was happy to be part of his children's lives. What was different about this man? Hochschild argued that he had reflected on gender roles and decided to accept only that part of masculinity that fit in his life. The other more oppressive forms of masculinity (the kind that would make a man feel "less than" if he cares for his children), he chose to reject. Here is the essence of Hochschild's analysis, which she built into a theory about gender roles, gender role awareness, and the taking or forsaking of domestic responsibilities. Outliers can give ethnographers immense insight into why a pattern has emerged.

Answering "So What?"

The "so what" question is the most important aspect to ethnography. It is what differentiates ethnography from journalism. As an ethnographer, you must use your data reduction, visualization, and tools of drawing conclusions to explain what a given phenomenon means to participants.

When I was in journalism school, we had a professor named Michael who loved to remind us of his time at the venerable *Toronto Star*. "Hemingway worked for The Star. Wrote a fantastic story about a fire," he'd say, with a faraway look in his eye. Michael himself once had an editor who routinely rejected his stories for lacking relevance. The editor would read the story and look at Michael and ask the simple question, "What does it mean to Metro?" "Metro" referred to metro Toronto. Michael's failure was to tell the readers why they should care about the story. I often remind myself this when I'm preparing my final report. "What does it mean to Metro?" I ask myself. "Metro," in this case, means my client's product or strategy.

What does the emergence of digital note taking "mean to Metro"? It depends on what "Metro" is. If your client is a paper notebook company, then digital note taking may mean, "We need a new business model." If your company sells cloud-based data storage, digital note taking means a potentially new business model. If your company already sells a digital note-taking tool, you must work harder. Students insist they take notes, when in reality they do not. What does this mean? It means your product must give its customers a sense of security, and the ability to "feel good" about using it.

The best way to prepare to answer the "what does it mean to Metro" question is to read widely. Understand the landscape of your client's product space, but also understand social life in general. Make constant connections back to social theory in your everyday life. Notice social activity in public places and ask yourself, "So what? What does it mean to Metro?" Practice interpreting what you witness through the lens of Goffman's theory of the presentation of self, or Butler's notion that gender is a performance. Apply Bourdieu's idea of cultural capital while you window shop. Some people are more naturally gifted at interpretation and analysis than others, but all people can become better through regular practice.

I eventually finished my master's thesis. My analysis was adequate, but certainly not groundbreaking. I did practice applying social theories to what I witnessed, and I learned how to reduce data before I began analysis. Looking back, I would not change that experience, even though some of my earlier conclusions I now find cringe-worthy. You, too, must go through the phase of being out of your depth and overwhelmed with data. Eventually, you will improve.

Chapter 10
Reporting

There is a measure of heartbreak in fieldwork. All the places you go and all the people you meet fill your mind and your heart with stories, good and bad, wonderful and tragic. The typical ethnographer wallows in these stories throughout fieldwork, telling and re-telling them. But there comes a moment when you must abandon some of these stories. You must filter out those which are not related to your research questions. You must leave them on the cuttingroom floor. Not everything you see and hear gets put in the final report. Not everyone you meet gets to meet your clients or stakeholders. It's a gift to hear these stories and meet these people, and it's tough to leave them behind when the project is over.

Research reports have a dubious reputation for making very little impact in the private sector. Many reports are ushered unceremoniously to the proverbial shelf, immediately upon completion. Other reports, like one featured in the television show *Mad Men*, face an even less hospitable fate. *Mad Men* focuses on the American advertising industry in the 1960s and takes its name from Madison Avenue, the center of the industry at that time. This "golden age of advertising" marked the beginning of systematic attempts to understand consumers (Tunstall, 1964). In one scene in the first season, the gifted creative director Don Draper responds to a research report. Don sits at his desk with a dour look on his face. In front of him is what looks to be a 50-page, typewritten dossier. Across from him sits the researcher, a vaguely European, older woman wearing a suit. Don calls her "Miss." She corrects him, with a crisp, slightly accented "Doctor." She explains to him that cigarette smokers have a Freudian death wish, and that he should leverage this sublimated desire for death in his creative work for *Lucky Strike* cigarettes (the agency's biggest and most lucrative account). Don abruptly dumps the report in the trash can next to his desk. Her eyes follow the report's descent. That is the end of her research project.

This brief scene encapsulates everything that's wrong with research reporting in the private sector today. The researcher is erudite, but defensive. The report is flat and unengaging. The insights are unfamiliar and lack credibility. The client is outright hostile. The real casualty is the report itself, which garners exactly five minutes of attention. For the record, I'm more of a Jungian than a Freudian so I might like to attribute this report's fate to its school of psychological thought. But I would be fooling myself. It wasn't because the researcher chose the "wrong" theory, but because she took Don's hostility as an attack on her research ability and intelligence, and failed to understand how dull and uninviting her research appeared. I, too, have been guilty of such vanity, as are many ethnographers. We don't fail because we are not intelligent or erudite enough; we fail because we don't present our stakeholders with engaging material that will improve their ideas. We choose the medium which makes *us* feel comfortable, not the one our stakeholders would prefer. Don's role as creative director is to come up with ideas, and the researcher's report did nothing to spark any creativity in Don. It deserved its fate.

I take this interaction as a lesson almost every time I prepare an ethnographic report. How can I discourage my own "Don Draper" from throwing my report in the trash? How can I tempt him to ask me more about my research? What would it take for "Don" to come to me later with follow-up questions?

Traditionally, ethnography has produced one type of report: the book. In his book, *Tales from The Field*, esteemed ethnographer Van Maanen (2003) simply assumes that an ethnographer is a writer; he doesn't even consider other types of reporting in his analysis of ethnographic practice. In academic circles, there *simply is no other kind of reporting*. The intended audience is a group of other ethnographers. Perhaps the occasional quantitative social researcher might browse the book, but for the most part, academics write for each other, not for Don Draper. In the private sector, by contrast, there are many Don Drapers, just waiting to toss our book-length monographs into the trash. This chapter is about understanding what Don and his ilk really need from our craft, and how to create the ideal report to serve him and his creative needs.

Elements of Good Ethnographic Reports

In their study of a technology spin-off company, Alvesson and Sveningsson (2008) detail the organizational hijinks that ensue after a company decides to "create a culture." As external consultants and observers, they note that what began as a *process* of instilling cultural norms rapidly became simply the *procedure* of producing a document. In the end, the organization's leaders produced what they called "a culture" but was really PowerPoint presentations and Word documents that described the organization's ideal state. The entire project of cultural change became reified into the document itself. Research reports face the same potential pitfall of becoming simply a document instead of a *process of change*. Ethnography can transform organizational practice, but only if it elicits a new frame of thinking or empathy among members of the organization. An ethnographer may set out to uncover unmet consumer needs, but might end up simply producing a document that describes consumer complaints with the company's product. Predictably, such a report becomes a "tone deaf" artifact, out of step with the company's given product mythology, and relegated to trash cans everywhere. Worse still, the insights about real people and their real frustrations remain unknown and unanswered. Ethnographers must avoid this fate by making their ethnographic reports several things.

First, the report must be dramatic. By dramatic, I don't mean startling or sentimental. I mean that the report must contain the dramatic tension inherent to all good stories. Good stories will capture the imagination of your stakeholders. You may remember Freytag's Pyramid, the famous diagram that many of us learned when we studied short stories, novels, and plays. Freytag argued that the dramatic elements of a story are what coheres our understanding, makes the ideas intelligible, and most importantly, satisfies our salacious hunger for tension and its resolution.

The pyramid begins with setting the stage. The characters are introduced, and the audience learns about their lives, quirks, motivations. Russian playwright Anton Chekov famously remarked, "If in Act I you have a pistol hanging on the wall, then it must fire in the last act." His point was that ideas or objects introduced into the story must have a significance that is explained later in the story. Introduce only the details whose significance you plan to explain some time later in the story. Setting the stage leaves the audience wondering, "What next?"

Setting the stage is satisfyingly followed by the "inciting incident," or something that interrupts the set-up, such as a problem or sudden shift. The story then builds, with rising tension. The story reaches a climax at the top of the pyramid, only to lessen its fast pace in the "denouement." The story is tied up with a neat resolution at the end. Ethnographers that produce reports without any of these dramatic elements are producing dull portraits of human experience. Van Maanen (2003) acknowledges that this is a key element in writing good ethnography reports.

The dramatic ethnographic report will introduce the participants (the "characters") and the research site (the "setting"). This is typically the descriptive aspect of the report, in which quantitative researchers tend to use measures of central tendency and dispersion. Ethnographers may use cohering metaphors or customer journeys. Perhaps there are "pistols hanging on the wall" in this stage, such as a never-ending flood of email, or the daily frustration of traffic. Whatever the "pistol" is, it ought to be referred to later in the story, usually at the "inciting incident," which describes a problem, frustration, or unmet consumer need. The tension around this problem builds until ultimately the ethnographer describes how the participant negotiates the problem. Perhaps he chooses a competitor's product. Perhaps he is delighted with an upgrade. Perhaps he has lied to himself about his ability to cope with his problem, and buys a product to distract from his angst. The tension lowers and the participants manage to make sense of their choices until ultimately they have a new starting place, however imperfect it might be. It is in this section that good ethnographic reports provide interpretation and answer the question "so what?" If consumers are buying products to cope with their angst, what does this mean? It means there is an opportunity to reduce their angst through a better designed product, through a simpler service,

Figure 5: Freytag's Pyramid of Dramatic Structure

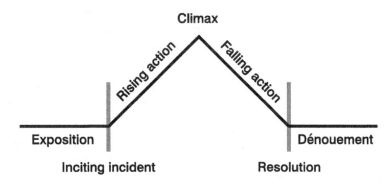

through a more empathetic customer support program. It might also mean that a company could take advantage of this dissociative tendency and feed consumers' needs to hide from themselves, cravenly pocketing the profits from this deceit. Individuals must decide what set of values they want the company to embody.[1] This dramatic structure can be used repeatedly, in an almost fractal manner. Good ethnographic reports are filled with a series of mini-stories, each introducing equal measures of tension and resolution.

The second criterion of a good ethnographic report is that it must be culturally consistent with the "truth regime" of the given organization. A "truth regime" is a coherent system of epistemic claims on truth used within a given culture (Weir, 2008). Organizations have culturally specific ways of representing and acknowledging the truth. Scientific truth is a type of truth common to most contemporary corporations. Scientific truth is spoken by "authorities" or those who are somehow credentialed to speak the truth, and non-truth is considered "error," not simply lying. By contrast, "mundane," or everyday truth can be spoken by anyone, its validity is readily apparent because it was observed, and non-truth is in fact lying. In our example from *Mad Men*, Don discounts the researcher's truth as unbelievable. What he is really doing is asserting the dominance of mundane truth over scientific truth. He doesn't care about her carefully researched argument that people have a death wish; he believes people smoke because they enjoy it, not because they want to die. Don finds the researcher's conclusions incredible because so many people smoke and it's hard to believe they all have a death wish. Her conclusions might have been scientifically "true" or valid, in that she followed scientific procedures, but Don's everyday observations contradict this truth. He doesn't care how "valid" her science is; he simply does not believe her truth.

This sort of "truth game" happens all the time. People jockey for dominance by asserting the verisimilitude[2] of their claims and decrying rival claims that use other truth regimes. Weir (2008) argues that the drive to teach creationism in schools, under the banner of "intelligent design," is really just symbolic or religious truth attempting to battle it out with scientific truth. Donna Flynn's study of ethnography at Microsoft was similar; ethnographers attempted to assert the scientific truth of their study, while program managers disputed its scientific validity. Ethnographers must attune themselves to their clients' truth regime and craft their report with that in mind. A report prepared for Microsoft or NASA might entail charts, graphs, and evidence of scientific practice, as would be culturally expected and accepted in that organization. But that exact same report will likely fall flat if presented to senior managers at *Cirque du soleil*. What is considered "true" in theatre is not reducible to charts or graphs. Imagine the absurd scene if a researcher were to assert that one circus character was "better" than another because of some sort of scientific truth. Good character development is self-evident to anyone watching the show, and is not intelligible in the scientific truth regime. Knowing your stakeholders' truth regime, and matching it, is a critical step in avoiding the dreaded trash can.

Ethnographic reports are generally more akin to mundane truth than scientific truth. Stories are readily apparent, particularly if they include direct quotes, audio, or video clips. Many people in the private sector will consider the typical ethnographic report as "error" because of its small sample size. This is where you must contradict that contention by documenting (and counting) the sheer numbers of interactions, objects, conversations, and behaviors that you did observe. Moreover, you must appeal to the mundane truth that most private-sector managers still implicitly uphold, even as they purport to accept the preeminence of scientific truth. Good stories have a way of recovering the dominance of this truth regime.

The third and final characteristic of a good ethnographic report is that it "lives beyond its form." By this I mean that the report itself is ultimately lifeless unless it manages to be taken up by its stakeholders in social interaction. Don Draper's report on consumers' smoking habits, for example, was part of exactly one social interaction before being ignored forever. The best reports are those that are talked about and referenced long after they are delivered. This is definitely a high bar to achieve, and sometimes it's more about luck and good timing than report quality. But there are steps ethnographers can take to ensure that their reports have a good chance of being talked about long after they are finished. Private-sector ethnographic reports are successful if they are dramatic and consistent with the organization's truth regime. But they become truly transformative if their ideas come alive in social interactions

One way to succeed at all three success criteria is to innovate the form of the report. Choose one in line with the organization's truth regime, but do not be afraid to push your clients and stakeholders with an unexpected but delightful alternative. Theatre professor Linda Hutcheon's (2006) book on adapting books and movies for the stage provides some lessons here. She documents the criteria for successful adaptations, such as adapting a book to a movie, a movie to a play, or even a video game to a movie. She argues that adaption is about embedding a delightful surprise into a familiar story. The best movie adaptations often feature a familiar character played by an unexpected but welcomed actor (think Dame Judi Dench playing "M" in the James Bond movies). The general frame of the story is maintained, its "bones" are recognizable and well crafted, but it has an unexpectedly delightful element to it that allows its audience to understand the topic in a new way. Your ethnographic report should be dramatically well composed, use the right truth regime, but also be slightly unexpected in its delivery. Here are a few ways to achieve this standard.

Written Reports

Documents

I still create old-fashioned documents created in Microsoft Word. Other private-sector ethnographers are sometimes surprised when I tell them this. There is a pervasive belief the people in the private sector no longer read. This is not true; people *are simply reading differently.* Shifts in reading habits happen at key historical moments. Around 1750, for example, people stopped reading small numbers of books deeply, and over and over again. They began to read more books but less deeply. People were not reading less after 1750, they were reading differently.

Today, people are actually reading more than in years past, but they are reading in shorter spurts, browsing for specific information or keywords, and integrating words with audio or video (Liu, 2005). It's no longer normal for marketing executives to pull out a book and start reading it. It's unusual to see engineers open books, unless it is to consult some reference material. Even physicians rarely pull out books anymore, relying increasingly on digital materials. But people read emails, Power Point decks, and Web sites. This form is shorter, more visual and more easily flipped through than your traditional document. But people still read in the private sector.

Documents can be created in such a way as to tempt even the busiest executive to read. In my years as a secretary way back in the early '90s, I learned one very valuable skill: how to use styles and outline view in Microsoft Word. To this day I use this process to sketch out my reports. Using a "style" heading will allow you to create tables of contents automatically. In the electronic version of the document, Word will also transform the table of contents into clickable hyperlinks. This document design better matches contemporary reading practice, which involves keyword spotting and less linear consumption. Such interactive documents are far more accessible to the contemporary executive because they allow the reader to select sections that are directly of interest. A liberal use of white space and diagrammatic elements will make the Word document appear more engaging, and less like a block of text. Your document should look more like a magazine article than a traditional academic paper.

Unlike Don Draper's researcher, I supplement my Word document with other, more engaging formats. This supplement is crucial, in that serves as a marketing campaign for the actual report. Ethnographers themselves often think it is normal to pick up a book, filled with blocks of text, and read it. Most people today do not; they must be convinced of the value of the text before they consider reading it. This may well be a sign of the future. In his recent dystopic novel, *Super Sad Love Story,*

Gary Shteyngart (2010) portrays books as a symbol of embarrassment. Characters who witness another reading a book often react with nervous giggling or hostile disapproval. It is evocative of the embarrassing topic of parenthood in *Brave New World*. Embarrassment about books could soon be part of popular culture, but even were that true, people would still read.

I often prepare a separate presentation, using PowerPoint, which I use to present the ideas in meetings. This is the "movie trailer" version of the deeper, more detailed report document. You may never be able to convince some people to read an old-fashioned ethnographic book, but you most definitely can convince your clients and stakeholders to read a well laid out Word document.

Personas are another useful complement to Word-based reports. Personas are archetypes, generated from actual qualitative data. There is no actual person underneath an individual persona; it is an amalgam of several participants. Personas are routinely used in the private sector to guide design. Unfortunately, they are often done badly. Steve Portigal's (2008) famous essay "Persona non grata" is a must-read. He argues that personas are often nothing more than stereotypes. But when done well, the persona is a useful way to summarize the voluminous amount of qualitative data.

Laid Out Documents

If you have the luxury of either knowing a layout program, like Adobe InDesign, or having a colleague with such skills, it's a wonderful way to lay out your insights in a visually appealing and attractive package. Tools like InDesign are what professional graphic artists use to lay out magazines, advertisements, and newspapers. It allows the layout artist more control over pagination, illustrations, and other design elements than Word does. It is the tool that most magazine art departments use to lay out their magazines today. But InDesign has a steep learning curve, so I have yet to attempt an entire layout process myself. Most ethnographers will lack the technical and design skills needed to use InDesign to its best potential. But fortunately, there are many graphic designers that are deeply familiar with InDesign and who work on a freelance basis.

The kinds of reports best suited to a laid-out format are those that have sufficient visual elements. Diagrams, photographs, and illustrations are key to making a laid-out document worth the extra cost of a designer. One note of caution on this kind of layout: do not underestimate the time it takes to edit and lay out the document. It is not sufficient to simply hand off the text to the designer. Often, text must edited or deleted to fit a given layout, something most ethnographers would prefer to do themselves. For this reason, I have spent countless hours sitting next to graphic designers, collaborating on writing headlines, determining placement of pictures, and deleting superfluous text. This time is well spent, in the end, because such reports look and feel like a magazine. But it takes a significant amount of time.

Both laid-out documents and word-processing documents benefit from professional printing. Selecting a slightly more expensive paper stock provides a palpable level of quality to the report, giving it its best chance of being read and shared among your clients and stakeholders. The paper stock, the illustrations, and the layout all communicate the value of the document itself. A double-spaced document, filled with text and printed unceremoniously on plain white paper makes the report appear to be a mere commodity. Spend the time creating your report, for when you present the report, it should appear to be worth the wait (this is its dramatic element, embodied).

Visual Reports

Presentations

In contemporary corporate life, digital presentation "documents" are ubiquitous. These are sometimes in the form of Keynote but are usually in the form of PowerPoint. Few software programs have both the dominance and dubious distinction of PowerPoint. In his famous essay, "The Cognitive Style of PowerPoint," statistician Edward Tufte (2003) rails against its power to stultify thought. He argues that the default templates in PowerPoint box our thinking into simplistic, analytically imprecise categories, which, when arranged in the nested bulleted lists, falsely suggest a hierarchy of ideas. He also argues that the typical slide's information density is so low that it forces us to create too many slides to convey everything we want to convey. Many of us have witnessed this phenomenon firsthand, when a presenter has one hour, but well over 60 slides in the deck. It's as if we all forgot that PowerPoint is a *presentation* tool, and not a document-creation tool.

Tufte is correct of course; any original creative endeavor could never rely solely on pre-fabricated templates to adequately communicate its unique contribution. Imagine if we took this same approach with words. You have a uniquely clever essay you wish to publish, and in order to do so, you follow a templated paragraph style which always begins with the same phrase. This is essentially what PowerPoint templates do to original contributions.

But all that said, PowerPoint can also be used to present research in dramatic and engaging ways. Most academic PowerPoint users fail to use its diagrammatic elements, which can greatly enhance it. The secret is to recognize, and truly accept, that PowerPoint decks are not intended to be "documents" that are read at one's leisure. They are *accompaniments* to other documents.

PowerPoint is so ubiquitous in the private sector that few people even question its use. But question it you should, if you want your research to garner the time and attention it deserves. This means accepting that there is no such thing as a "reading deck." There is no such thing as a set of PowerPoint slides that can adequately substitute for a book, document, or article. PowerPoint cannot replace a book, document, or article; this does not and cannot happen. So if you find yourself jamming text into PowerPoint slides, stop. Slide after slide of bulleted lists not only bores your audience members, it also serves as a poor advertisement for the "real" report that you are hoping they one day read. But because of its ubiquity, PowerPoint is culturally expected. Those who do not create a PowerPoint deck may be perceived to be out of touch with contemporary cultural practices. You simply must have a PowerPoint deck, but you do not need to have it be the totality of your insight. Communicate to your clients and stakeholders that the PowerPoint deck is a visual artifact, and that there is more insight in the text-based report. Advise them that the PowerPoint presentation is no substitute for the deeper analysis. Give them the top-level PowerPoint summary of what the report itself says, but do not make this summary a mess of text.

Figure 6: Excerpt from a Graphic Novel Report
Courtesy of Copernius Consulting Group Inc.

Graphic Novels

Graphic novels, also known as "comic books," have garnered a new reputation as a legitimate narrative form. The form is popular because the images convey emotional information quickly and artfully. They are easy to "read" in that there is little actual text. In Edward Tufte's language, they are "information dense." They have become so much a part of our cultural life that they are routinely transformed into movies, either in the familiar superhero genre, or the more satirical *Scott Pilgrim* anti-hero genre. The graphic novel has truly arrived as a storytelling form.

Graphic novels are a wonderful way to represent the ethnographer's field notes, particularly when video or still photos are not possible. There are many instances where recording video is unethical or outright illegal. For example, patient-physician interaction is a deeply intimate and private interaction that is governed by privacy laws. Even if an ethnographer ethically and legally navigates this interaction, the video camera itself is a very intrusive presence. Using the old-fashioned pen-and-paper in this kind of situation is not only legally and ethically more sound, it also produces better insight. This is precisely the kind of situation that can be turned into a graphic novel.

There are plenty of reasons why ethnographers may shy away from the graphic novel, but none of them is insurmountable. First, and perhaps most practically, few ethnographers have the illustration skills to draw a 30- or 40-page comic book. Second, ethnographers may consider the visual form to be less dense or analytically precise than the text-based form. Neither of these reasons presents an insurmountable problem. Illustrators can be hired via the web, and decent tools now exist to share large data files over the web. Hiring a freelance illustrator can be relatively painless, provided that the ethnographer has a clear description of key moments in his field study, actual quotes from participants, and a keen eye for environmental details. Ethnographers may also be surprised to learn that creating a graphic novel is just as analytically challenging as writing a text report. What qualifies as a key interaction? Which environmental details are significant? What participant quotes are the right ones to use? Suddenly, it appears that preparing a graphic novel is the same process as writing a text-based report; only the medium has changed.

There is one key difference between an ethnographic graphic novel and a fictional one. Ethnography is about description and explanation, so a graphic representation of ethnographic research must provide both. Simply describing the scenes or summarizing what was said is not sufficient. Your graphic novel must also explain the meaning of the interactions. What does it mean that a patient and his wife bicker about his smoking habits? What is the significance of the patient-physician language barrier? What should your client know about this interaction, from a design, innovation, or marketing perspective? Graphic novels must answer the question, "so what?" just like every other report.

Video Documentaries

Most private-sector ethnographers use video today, whether it is the right medium or not. There are several reasons why video is the most popular report medium. First, there is a pervasive belief that clients and stakeholders do not read (a myth, which I have debunked throughout much of this book). Second, advancements in video recording technology have made it significantly easier and cheaper to record video. Cameras are smaller and cheaper and require less expertise to actually use (however, video editing still requires significant expertise and equipment). The final reason why video has become *de rigueur* for private-sector ethnography is that clients have become habituated to it. Purchasers of market research have been receiving video reports for many years, starting with the grainiest focus-group video tapes from the 1980s. Clients may ask for video reports without realizing there are other media, and ethnographers may simply provide video because clients have asked specifically for it. Video has become so synonymous with ethnography that some market research companies are selling "ethnography" services, which are really just video diaries, recorded by participants themselves.

Novice ethnographers must know that video production is difficult, expensive, and time-consuming. My friend and fellow ethnographer Bruno Moynié would be the first to tell you. Bruno has specialized in ethnographic filmmaking for 20 years, having made dozens of ethnographic films for private-sector clients. His equipment includes a broadcast-quality video camera, a few backup cameras, several wireless microphones, and a home editing studio with two large monitors, a tower computer, and a separate air-conditioning unit to keep the entire room from over-heating. Video production is not for the faint of heart.

When to Use Video

There are certain kinds of private-sector ethnographic projects that lend themselves easily to a video report. Ethnographies that involve the manual handling of products are ideal. For example, if your product requires assembly of any sort, your clients and stake holders need to know how well their assembly works. Alternatively, your clients may need to know what a domestic or workplace scene actually looks like in order for their product to be designed correctly. If you are designing a physical device, for example, having video will help your design team match the spatial dimensions and aesthetic style of consumers' homes or offices. Video is ideal for such situations. Projects that have a sufficient budget for hiring a separate videographer and/or video editing are also worth investing in the video.

Video is not always worth it. Digital software design projects, for example, might only need a video component of the participant's face while using the product to convey adequately the emotional impact of poor usability. But a complete video summary of the interview with the participant is not necessary. Using video in this case may actually compromise the quality of the report, if the researcher devotes more time to video editing than to actual analysis.

Audio Reports

Radio is perhaps the most underestimated storytelling medium today. Radio news programs, such as NPR's *This American Life,* have far more impact than most people realize. Well told radio stories convey the emotion and drama needed to elicit empathy in your clients and stakeholders, yet few if any ethnographers employ this medium. This is likely because radio documentary making is a specialized skill, usually confined to radio journalists. But just as with video production, the tools have come down in price and complexity, so audio reports offer a wonderfully rich and relatively less intrusive data collection process than video.

Podcasts

The podcast is the Cadillac of audio reports, in that it may involve mixing multiple interviews, background noise, and narration. Just as with video production, this is not for the faint of heart. But its results can be dramatic and engaging. The bonus with the podcast is that stakeholders can listen to the report while they drive or commute. The average commute time in the United States is 25 minutes, and in Canada it is 26 minutes (McKenzie, 2011; Statistics Canada, 2011). Your stakeholders are a captive audience while commuting, and your report, if crafted well and offered in the correct format, will make your participants come alive. Stakeholders will not "read a report" but be invited into your participants' worlds.

To make the podcast, you must first have adequate recording devices. This means going beyond the audio from your Livescribe pen (incidentally, I happen to know that the Livescribe also tends to record the scribbling sounds of you writing your notes; this is a non-starter for the podcast). Good quality audio for the interviews, some clips of ambient noise, and potentially some licensed or Creative Commons-licensed music will give you the inputs for an engaging audio podcast. Mixing these elements requires both good editing skills and the right software. Unfortunately, freelance radio editors are not as prevalent as illustrators or videographers, but they do exist. If you decide you'd like a podcast, it is worth doing it correctly.

Audio Slideshows

Audio slideshows are much easier for novices than are podcasts. They involve simply creating a slideshow and either adding music automatically over top, or recording yourself narrating and describing the still photos. Tools of this category allow you to sync sounds with pictures precisely. SoundSlides Plus allows you to sync your audio to a set of PowerPoint slides, and to export the entire package into a convenient HTML5 package, which you can burn to a DVD or post to a public or private web site. I have used this format as the "takeaway" or handout portion of my research. This format is both as familiar as PowerPoint and as information dense as radio. The ability to export it makes it possible to hand it out or share it to stakeholders who are unable to attend your presentation (which happens frequently in the private sector). Such slideshows also tend to live on outside your Word report of the final presentation, making it an ideal format for conveying ethnographic insight to those unfamiliar with the method.

Reports That Aren't Reports

Most ethnographers would intuitively understand that a report that is simply handed over, no matter how well prepared, is not going to come alive. Having your ethnographic report "live beyond its form" necessarily entails architecting one (if not a series of them) social interaction that makes the research its primary topic. In most private-sector organizations, this means designing and facilitating in-person meetings that focus on the ethnographic findings. This is especially powerful when stakeholders come along on ethnographic interviews with the researcher. Clients that have witnessed a consumer's frustration first-hand are the ethnographer's greatest ally in her effort to make her report come alive. Going along on the fieldwork is only the first step; clients must be guided through the research and analysis process in order for them to truly internalize the ethnographic empathy.

Collaborative Analysis Sessions

The challenge that most ethnographers face in enlisting their clients as co-researchers is that their clients are not usually trained in ethnographic methods, and are therefore not equal partners in the data collection and analysis process. Clients should not be equal to the ethnographer, but they should be welcomed on the journey, given the tools they need to succeed, and guided through the process of cognitive transformation that ethnography so often brings. Collaborative analysis sessions, which are finely architected and carefully facilitated, are one way to do this.

Group analysis sessions can fall victim to being dominated by the most forceful personality, just as focus groups can be. The ethnographer must shift from being researcher to being facilitator by identifying and guiding all the personalities in the room toward the working conclusions she has already identified. This is very difficult to do without any training in facilitation or teaching, and it's well advised to enlist the help of a note-taker or colleague to help move furniture, re-arrange Post-it notes, and stave off problems in group dynamics. The ethnographer should also enlist the help of the primary client stakeholder; the primary stakeholder's responsibility is to provide insight into group function (or dysfunction) and become a co-owner of the outcomes.

A collaborative analysis session should be held in a large, open room with ample wall space. Do not attempt to conduct such a session with a large, immovable conference table in the middle; you will find quickly that it invites participants to sit and not participate. The ethnographer's role here is to create a space for participants to share their experiences in the field, and to guide them through drawing conclusions that will be accepted collectively. In a sense, the only outcome the ethnographer should aim for is a general sentiment of consensus, not necessarily the "right" conclusions. To achieve this, it is critical to have a detailed, minute-by-minute agenda that the ethnographer, note-taker, and primary stakeholder have devised. Before having such a session, it's a good idea to know what general themes you would like to have emerge, based on your training and experience as an ethnographer. The challenge is bringing the group to those very themes. This is why such sessions are best conducted by experienced facilitators or teachers.

Plays

Doctor Yvette Lu is a Vancouver-based family physician. She trains medical students on the experience of a chronic illness, but she does not lecture them, or take them on tours of such patients' homes. Instead, Dr. Lu performs a series of monologues, on stage (she moonlights as an actor, director, and producer). The monologues are a product of her own interviews with three patients coping with chronic illness. She has synthesized the major themes into a single "character." Designers would recognize Dr. Lu's character as a "design persona." Her audience learns about the major challenges such patients experience. Dr. Lu's goal with this process is to give these medical students a deep understanding of what chronic illness does to a person. In other words, Dr. Lu is teaching empathy.

Perhaps surprisingly, Dr. Lu's monologues have been requested repeatedly and have had an impact on medical students' understanding of what it means to have a chronic illness. "At the end, I felt like I knew someone inside and out...her feelings, ideas, needs, and expectations," medical student Alvin Ip told University of British Columbia's *Trek* magazine. "[It] reminded me of how important it is to not only treat the disease, but also comfort...the patient." What an ethnographer wouldn't give to hear his client say something similar! Plays are indeed a difficult form of reporting; Dr. Lu is a professional actor and director. But given the right combination of people and practices, they can be massively influential.

Why I Did Not Include "Brainstorming"

Brainstorming has a bad name, not because it's a bad idea (there are no bad ideas!), but because it's mistakenly believed to lack structure. Good brainstorming is painstakingly planned and executed. It has a bad name because few people recognize that the key to "unstructured" play is, paradoxically, to add constraints. All too often, brainstorming descends into a series of undirected conversations, with little to show for it. For this reason, I discourage the use of brainstorming in ethnography, unless—and this is a very big unless—the ethnographer is experienced running brainstorming games and techniques. Such tools as "Gamestorming"(www.gogamestorm.com) are worth investigating if you wish to add structure to your brainstorm methods. But unless you have a tightly organized and firmly grounded plan, I advise most people to leave brainstorming off the agenda.

Don Draper is not a fan of unstructured thinking, as much as he might argue otherwise. Watching him over six years of *Mad Men*, I've begun to form a clear opinion of his use of research. Don is an amateur anthropologist. He understands stories, narrative, culture, and practices. He designed his Kodak "carousel" campaign based on his own unsystematic autoethnography of the bittersweetness of family, nostalgia, and attachment. He even used culture to guide what ultimately became the *Lucky Strike* slogan, "They're toasted." Don's affinity for cultural expression and human emotion is what drives him to adopt or discard insights about the consumer. Private-sector ethnographers can take a page from Don when preparing their reports. Their aim should be to tell human stories within cultural context. That way, they are likely to hear their reports being discussed rather than sitting on a shelf or being sent to the trash.

Chapter 11
Beyond Ethnography

In his study of motorcycle clubs in 1960s Birmingham, British sociologist Paul Willis (1978) paid special attention to a consumer product: the motorcycle. The "bike boys," as he calls them, use their motorcycles as a kind of language, to communicate their views of the world. The motorcycle is a tool they use to express themselves, by modifying the motorcycle in particular ways. Writing in his later book, *The Ethnographic Imagination* (2000), Willis explains how the bike boys use their motorcycles as a means of expression: "Choosing carefully between different bikes; removing baffles from exhaust; adding chrome; fitting a cattle horn or different-style handle bars; the style of riding; the refusal to wear crash helmets: all of these were 'material variables' open to creative manipulation by the bike boys to enhance the expressive meaning of the bike" (p. 25). The motorcycle becomes a medium for the bike boys to tell the world how they feel.

The "ethnographic imagination" is about seeing products and services through this cultural lens. It is an analytic that sees products and services not just as objective "things" but as symbols people employ to "talk" to the rest of the world. The ethnographic imagination is about understanding that people use products to give off a strategic, architected impression that they themselves may not even consciously realize. People use products to adorn themselves, to show their social conscience, to demonstrate their moral superiority, to cement their membership in a group, or to reject a social role foisted upon them. Those in the private sector who have the ethnographic imagination see this language, decode its symbols, and use it to create better products and services that people want or need.

Product managers, designers, and market researchers with the ethnographic imagination believe the meaning of our social world is not a given. They take the participant's "standpoint." Using the ethnographic imagination means looking for regularity, cyclicality, and ritual in everyday life. It means seeing rule-following and rule-breaking as two sides of the same analytic coin. It means noticing mundane activities not as mere wallpaper, but as the very fabric that binds people into groups, organizations, and even nations. This way of looking at the world is not based on merely the "data" of people's stories, but on the way in which you investigate people and the products and services they use.

This realization means liberation. It means you are free to take the best of the ethnographic method and apply it to other research methods. Purists, of course, will disagree with this. The academic ethnographer may insist on a year's fieldwork, even if it isn't possible or necessary. The private-sector purist will disavow anything other than field-based research, even if field-based research is logistically impossible. I am not a proponent of purity of method, but of the piety of a consumer-centric worldview. This piety means you place the consumer's thoughts, wishes, desires, and shames in the center of your approach, regardless of the method. The ethnographic imagination can be applied to almost all research methods because it is a school of thought more than a pure method.

This chapter is about applying the ethnographic imagination to other types of methods, including online research, literature reviews, focus groups, and classic lab usability studies. The challenge with these methods is that their very design privileges the researcher's perspective over the participant's. Unlike fieldwork, these other methods allow the researcher to control the interactions with participants. This kind of control lends itself to an etic point of view, even if the researcher wishes to avoid it. In the field, the ethnographer follows the participant's everyday activities. But in a lab or focus group room, the researcher often tightly controls the agenda, directs the participants to particular topics, and even controls seemingly mundane details like the temperature of the room or the height of the chairs. Even with an awareness of this power, the researcher can easily fail to see the participant's perspective, simply because the tone of control has been set by the very design of the research site.

The focus group room's two-way mirror is a metaphor for this shift in favor of the researcher. Researchers, clients, and stakeholders can watch participants (and even enjoy tasty snacks!) as if they were zoo animals on display. The usability lab is even more off-putting. It is equipped with both a two-way mirror and complex technology, which participants will neither understand nor be able to see through. The researcher stands behind the proverbial "curtain" while participants are expected to offer up insights. It's an environment that puts the power squarely in the hands of the researcher, and makes it that much more difficult to see the world from the consumer's perspective. The researcher controls the room, and the participant is a guest there. But even in these locations, the ethnographic imagination can guide the private-sector ethnographer to conduct ethnographic investigations that put the consumer first.

Ethnographic Literature Reviews

The literature review is the unsung hero of private-sector market research in general. The positivist bias inside most contemporary corporations leads to a preference for original, empirical research over the summary of other researchers' work. This bias results in expensive and sometimes unnecessary research. Private-sector ethnographers in particular are often guilty of this because their very craft is an embodied, tacit skill that is practiced "in the field." Somehow, gathering and synthesizing other people's ethnographic findings seems antithetical to being an actual ethnographer.

I encourage all ethnographers to re-evaluate this position. In the roughly two centuries of ethnographic research, there is always a piece of research that is relevant to your precise research question. And there are several pieces of research that can be inferentially relevant. Private-sector ethnography is about making better products and services for people, and this can only be assisted by knowing more about people.

Table 8: Selected Academic Journals Featuring Ethnographic Research

Journal	Description	Available through
Journal of Consumer Culture	Interpretivist marketing research journal with robust theoretical debates on the cultural nature of many products and services	Sage Journals
Ephemera	Journal of cultural studies, focusing on politics, social media, movies, music, and other cultural products	Free online: www.ephemerajournal.org/
Critical Quarterly	Journal of cultural studies focusing on literary criticism, film, and television	Wiley Online Library
EPIC Proceedings	Proceedings of the Ethnographic Praxis in Industry Conference	AnthroSource
Human Computer Interaction	Technology-focused journal with some ethnographic research	Taylor and Francis Online Journals
Design Management Review	Design journal featuring design theory and some ethnographic research	Available to Design Management Institute members
Sociology	Sociological journal with some empirical ethnographic research	Sage Journals
IEEE Xplore	Collection of journal articles and conference proceedings, some of which focus on user experience and system design	ieeexplore.ieee.org/Xplore/home.jsp

Literature reviews are unfortunately hampered by the paywall system of academic publishing. Many of the best journals are too costly for companies to purchase for the only occasional need. But some of these journals are available through public libraries.

A good ethnographic literature review focuses on the cultural aspects of a given product or service. What are the behaviors relating to this product space? What are the beliefs about this product space, or the identity experience of those who typically use it? Such research can give product designers good hunches as to where to best aim their designs, but of course it will not give precise answers to such question as, "How many buttons should I add to this tool?" or "What color should I make this?"

Online Ethnography

As early as 2000, researcher Christine Hine produced a comprehensive book on doing ethnography on the web. Her book, *Virtual Ethnography* (2000), lays out a clear and analytically precise method for doing ethnographic research on the web. Hine argues that the web is indeed a "place," just like a house, office, or a shopping mall. The challenge that most researchers have in studying the web, however, is using the same analytical categories of physical places.

Hine points out that there the researcher must identify the limits of the "site" of research in online research. Novice ethnographers may simply identify "the web" as the site of study, but this is just as vague as identifying "the world" as a place to study. Instead, Hine argues that the researcher must be specific about the virtual location of study. In contemporary terms, this is a bit easier than when Hine was originally writing, in that communities have coalesced and become more identifiable on the web today. Online social networking sites (SNSs) have discrete user bases and identifiable "locations" on the web. Just as field ethnographer may identify a particular company's workplace and the workers who work there as a site of research, the online ethnographer can now identify a particular SNS and its user base as a site of study. Hine herself demonstrated this in her earlier research, looking at bulletin boards and online fora. Today it is much easier simply to identify a single social network, such as LinkedIn, or even a subsection of a network, such as an individual Facebook group.

More contemporary examples of ethnographic work in the virtual space include Rob Kozinets's (2010) work on "netnography." Kozinets is the chair of marketing at the Schulich School of Business at York University. His approach is extremely useful for those who work in the private sector and focus on digital experiences. Advertising planners, interaction designers, and qualitative market researchers can all learn from this basic approach. Kozinets applies the lens of culture to discrete online spaces, just as Hine suggests. His particular focus is interpreting the marketing implications from online communities. The essential element of Kozinets's approach is focusing on the cultural expressions in the online space. He points out that the major advantages of using the online medium include the ability to look backward in time (the web is a massive archive) and the ability to reach many geographic areas without travel. Researchers using the web as their primary site of research can now also elicit responses directly from real people. On today's web, that is likely as easy as finding a forum or several fora that focus on the topic of interest. The researcher must be systematic about the choice of community and determine precisely which times and dates of posting she will sample. She must also have clear research questions that focus on the values, norms, and beliefs about, for example, home maintenance and renovation, likely with an eye to developing a theory around gender performance, or perhaps work and fulfillment. Dipping into a forum for a few hours, just to see what's going on, is not research. Having a clearly defined set of questions and a site of research will provide meaningful results, and moreover, will show your clients and stakeholders that you indeed have followed a systematic approach.

In her research on teens and social networking, danah boyd (2007) used an ethnographic lens to investigate a new kind of online destination: the social network site. Like Kozinets, boyd advocated mixing online and offline research methods. She achieved this through traditional participant observation with teenagers, ethnographic interviews with them about their online experiences, and the analysis and interpretation of online social network profiles. She found, among other things, that young people used social network sites to construct and perform identities. This wasn't "fieldwork" in the classic anthropological sense, but it offered a clear ethnographic, emic explanation of social life that just so happened to be online.

Today, there are a burgeoning number of companies that offer online community platforms specifically for the purpose of online qualitative research. Sixent and PluggedInCo are but two of these online focus group platforms. They are essentially designed as private, proprietary Facebook groups. These companies typically will recruit participants, from their list of users, based on your recruitment criteria. Depending on your research needs, you can request the participants to discuss a particular topic or complete a particular task. These platforms, used uncritically, can be quite deleterious to consumer-centric results because participants want to please their "clients" (that is, the researchers) and therefore may engage in pleasing behavior. This phenomenon, known well to researchers as "acquiescence bias," must be considered in the research design. Providing participants with a list of tasks to be completed engenders a spirit of service, not one of genuine opinions or naturalistic behavior. Ethnographers can still use these tools if they shape the research engagement as one of relatively less structure and more genuine observation. Asking participants to collect images they like from the web and to explain why they like them is sufficiently open ended to allow for creative self-expression. But asking participants to complete a step-by-step process is not ethnographic; it is a usability test (which of course has its merits, but it is not a cultural investigation in any way).

Adapting Ethnography for Focus Groups

Many ethnographers would be aghast at the suggestion that they abandon the field in favor of the focus group room. I personally would never recommend using focus groups over ethnography if the goal is to understand participants' lives deeply and meaningfully. That is not to say that focus groups are entirely useless, however, and it certainly doesn't mean that the use of a traditional focus group cannot improve the effectiveness of an ethnographic lens.

The focus group was popularized by sociologist Paul Lazarsfeld, who was a pioneer of applied social research. Lazarsfeld's research emerged at the time of the "mass audience" or the birth of a truly massive group of television viewers. His brand of applied sociology was of great interest to the emerging corporate power houses, the television networks. Lazarsfeld popularized the focus group (it had already existed, but his work made it a household name). Some might recognize Lazarsfeld's name from the Stanton-Lazarsfeld Analyzer, which is an instrument with dials that participants use to indicate approval or disapproval as they watch a program.

A variant of this machine is still used today, particularly during political debates or important speeches. Participants give real-time reactions to what the candidate is saying, and researchers can measure the impact of particular messages or phrases. Lazarsfeld introduced the focus group to this process, intending for participants to offer quick, simple opinions about clearly defined topics. The focus group is ideal for quickly communicated, simple opinions that do not fit neatly into a survey questionnaire. Indeed, that continues to be the main advantage of the focus group today—it provides consumers an opportunity to express these simple opinions in their own words.

But focus groups have well known limitations. The group can become easily dominated by a few, overwhelming voices; stronger personalities can easily drown out others. Focus groups are also ill suited to uncovering complex or experiential questions, such as "What is the essence of childhood play and game playing?" or "How do consumers navigate our customer service experience?" And of course, the main problem with focus groups is that they are a contrived setting that the researcher controls. The participants are "on display" for those behind the mirror. They are not in a naturalistic setting and are unlikely to engage in everyday behaviors with any authenticity whatsoever (Bryman, 2004).

Unfortunately, however, the focus group is also often used to answer complex, nuanced, and subtle consumer beliefs. It was never intended for this purpose, and is clearly not designed to provide such insight. Ethnographers and other researchers will note that beliefs are a cultural phenomenon, which is typically manifest in everyday behaviors. This is why field research and observation are required to have deep cultural understanding. No such everyday behavior is evident in the focus group room, making it perhaps the last place to uncover authentic, unpracticed, and genuine beliefs.

That said, however, there are times when a researcher does have a clear understanding of the topic area, and may even have secondary research that provides adequate understanding of everyday behaviors. There may also be a limitation of time and budget, making the focus group the preferred method. If you have an adequate understanding of the cultural landscape already, and if you have a clearly defined topic of interest, the focus group can provide insights. But the focus group must be embraced critically, with its limitations known, acknowledged, and mitigated.

Specifically, focus group moderators should engineer both the flow of the conversation and the physical space to put some of the power back into the hands of participants. To do this, the moderator should allow ample time for unstructured conversation about the values and beliefs participants have about the topic at hand. In all likelihood, this means sacrificing some of the desired moderation guide in favor of what participants feel is germane and important enough to bring to the table. The moderator should also abandon the traditional focus group room, with its zoo-like two-way mirror, in favor of a simple room with comfortable chairs, more like a living room than a sterile lab. It is even better to invite clients and stakeholders into this temporary living room and have them sit side-by-side with the participants. Sitting face-to-face with participants will make it more likely that clients will come to understand participants' experiences, in part because this kind of "body work," as technology researchers call it, demands a more intimate and engaged communication (Nardi and Whittaker, 2002). Snacks still can be served, but participants should share these snacks with the moderator and the clients. This again cements this as a "real" social interaction, more akin to field work than clinical study.

Why Usability Labs Can Never Be Ethnographic

Usability labs are not and cannot be sites of ethnographic research. It is impossible to understand a participant ethnographically in the usability lab because the need to understand a prototype's usability crowds out the ethnographic agenda. Some of my user experience colleagues may disagree with me on this point, but I argue that usability labs are fundamentally etic locations which cannot be altered or softened into the emic site that ethnographic research demands. There are several reasons why usability studies cannot be ethnographic.

First, it is far more difficult to have the usability lab study emulate more naturalistic social interactions. These labs are even more contrived, clinical places than focus group rooms. By their very design, usability labs make the research subject a piece of technology, not a topic, a person, or a culture. A usability researcher's job is to test how well real people can use a prototype technology. This goal is imprinted on the design of the lab itself, through built-in computer monitors and cameras pointed at the participant's face. Often times, participants are asked to speak aloud as they use a prototype, making the experience even more unnatural. This context makes it almost impossible for participants to act as they might on their home or office computer because it is so far removed from everyday experiences.

Second, and perhaps more important, the usability study's research agenda is at odds with the ethnographic imagination. The usability researcher asks: Can a user use this technology successfully? That is a specific research question that will do little to reveal participants' norms, values, and beliefs. There is simply too narrow a focus on the technology's usability to reveal any meaningful insights about a participant's cultural experience. Moreover, to answer the research question adequately, the usability researcher must wield a good measure of force in the course of the research, and continually direct the participant back toward the prototype. This is in direct opposition to the emic perspective and shifts the conversation away from what participants might feel important and toward their impressions of the prototype. They may genuinely believe that technology occupies no meaningful place in their lives. Their everyday behaviors may involve so many analogue tools that they probably never even attempt to use this new technology because they wouldn't stumble across it. Such findings can never be discovered in the usability lab because the original question about whether this prototype could be meaningful to participants is a foregone conclusion. Usability studies simply *assume* that the technology will be easily woven into people's established patterns of living, and that it will occupy some sort of meaningful place there. Ethnographic research, by contrast, considers this question of technology's integration still unanswered: Does technology mean anything important to these people? Could it possibly be part of their existing way of living? If so, where, when, and how? The usability researcher takes those questions as given, and begins the study from there.

Usability research is incredibly valuable to designing good technology (Kuniavsky, 2003). Ethnographers cannot offer the same insight into specific features and the functionality of technology itself. For this reason, I would never say ethnography should *replace* usability testing, but

I would caution anyone against attempting to use the usability lab to do ethnographic research. If your clients and stakeholders are demanding ethnography in a usability lab, there are likely many misperceptions about what research is and how it should add value to the corporate endeavor.

A Dedication to Ethnography

There is a Zen saying about the awareness one achieves when studying Zen Buddhism:

> First I saw a mountain.
> Then I saw there was no mountain.
> Then I saw a mountain.

This saying conveys the process one goes through when achieving a new level of insight. First, one is blind to the deeper essence of a thing (the mountain is just a mountain). Then one realizes that there is more to a thing than its appearance. There are so many human meanings layered upon that thing that it may feel that the thing doesn't even exist in the material world. It is just a fiction of our human creation. But eventually one realizes that there is still a thing. It exists, right there in front of you. No matter how much enlightenment you achieve, the thing is still there; it never disappears. Understanding how much human meaning we layer upon a thing changes our perception, but it does not change that the thing exists.

Once you have practiced ethnography in the private sector, it is likely that it will change you. You will no longer take traditional market research at face value. You will probably scoff at "mere statistics" and will knowingly believe you could find much more insight than a survey or a focus group. That may well be true in some cases, but it certainly is not true in all cases.

True ethnographic insight comes from the realization that all consumer behavior has human meaning layered on top of it. Most of this meaning is invisible to most people. Ethnographers are trained specifically to uncover this meaning. But they do themselves and their partners a disservice if they become arrogant about this skill. There is no room in the corporation for epistemological rigidity. There is no reason for ethnographers to believe their method is superior to other research methods.

It is easy to have such a belief system because ethnography is a luxury for most organizations. Only the most profitable corporations can afford to have in-house ethnographers, which makes most ethnographers outsiders by definition. In this role of professional stranger, it is tempting to privilege your own views over those of others. But if there is one way to best leverage ethnographic research, it is to have empathy not only for your participants, but also for your partners and stakeholders. Ethnography sometimes "makes the mountain disappear," but have faith; the mountain is still there, waiting for you.

Notes

Chapter 3

1 I use the word "perceived" here because I wish to indicate that this notion of time-scarcity is more of a cultural value than it is a reality. One is expected to acknowledge this perception in everyday practice in the private sector, which in turn perpetuates the perception, regardless of its empirical accuracy.

Chapter 4

1 Stuart Dreyfus notes there is also a sixth and final stage of learning he calls "expertise." Masters are able to choose a course of action quickly, but experts intentionally cross disciplinary lines to pick up new and innovative processes and knowledge. A classical pianist who studies jazz, and then brings back jazz-influenced rhythms to his classical interpretations, is an example of expertise.

2 I am a "cleaner," meaning I obsess over sorting and deleting old messages. As email volume increases, this strategy also fails, in that you can rarely keep up with the constant stream.

3 The academic ethnographer may also include access to proprietary databases of academic research, such as JSTOR. The use of these paywalled databases is somewhat controversial outside academia because their high subscription costs make them prohibitively expensive for the independent ethnographer, and even for some ethnographers embedded in large organizations. Google Scholar and Microsoft Academic Research can offer direct paths to PDFs freely available on the internet as one way of bypassing these paywalls. See Table 7.

4 Evernote was hacked in mid 2003, exposing millions of users' usernames and passwords. Evernote has an extra encryption option, which allows you to encrypt individual notes with an additional password, beyond the simple login password. It's worth bearing in mind that cloud-based tools are inherently vulnerable to privacy problems. Researchers should guard against putting any personally identifiable information (for example, first and last names, addresses, social insurance/social security numbers) all together in a single place.

Chapter 5

1 Check out the post here: thesocietypages.org/cyborgology/2013/08/21/selling-the-social-sciences/. I took the liberty of commenting, as did other social scientists working in applied fields.

Chapter 8

1 That said, however, Dreyfus concedes that one should not throw the baby out with the bathwater; virtual interaction is better than no interaction at all. Dreyfus's main point is that being physically co-located with another human being elicits an emotional reaction that is fundamentally embodied. Virtual interactions do not recreate this same visceral response, and can therefore never be equal to the face-to-face. Aspiring ethnographers who interact with participants through online channels should take note of this key difference, which I discuss further in the final chapter.

2 For more information about HIPAA, see this section of Department of Health and Human Services web site: www.hhs.gov/ocr/privacy/hipaa/understanding/summary/index.html

Chapter 9

1 Those of you who know Vancouver and its climate may immediately call foul at my description of a "sunny apartment." Why, this is *Vancouver*, you might say. There are no sunny apartments, only dark and rainy apartments. Perhaps it is the imperfections of my human memory, but I remember that apartment as one of the most blissful places I've ever lived. Doing a master's degree is perhaps the most enjoyable thing anyone could do, in that it is short, but the bar is high. You are surrounded by people better than you are, and you are expected to learn from them. My sunny apartment still is a symbol of that glorious time.

2 I find one of the major challenges in applied social research is the lack of familiarity with established social theory. I attribute this in part to an obsession with the present or very recent past. Research that is more than three years old is often considered so out-of-date that it may be irrelevant. That very well may be true if it is empirical research that relies heavily on current technology usage, which tends to get out of date very quickly. Theory, on the other hand, tends to answer questions with much longer shelf lives than empirical research. The more researchers remind their clients and stakeholders of theory's continuing relevance, the better the craft will be.

Chapter 10

1 The ethnographer may disagree with the craven choice, and it is their right to do so. How can such an ethnographer communicate such a position? By showing the cultural impact of choosing empty commercialism. What will the company embody? What will it represent? What kinds of consumers will this attract, and what kinds of employees?

2 Thanks to Catherine, my terrifyingly intelligent research methods professor, I can now plausibly use this word and in turn, terrify others.

References

Ader, L. N. (2011). Ethnography as Theory. *HAU: Journal of Ethnographic Theory, 1*(1), 211–219.

Agdal, R. (2005). Diverse and Changing Perceptions of the Body: Communicating Illness, Health, and Risk in an Age of Medical Pluralism. *Journal of Alternative and Complementary Medicine, 11 Suppl 1,* S67–75.

Alasuutari, P. (1995). *Researching Culture: Qualitative Methods and Cultural Studies.* Thousand Oaks, CA: Sage.

Alvesson, M., & Sveningsson, S. (2008). *Changing Organizational Culture: Cultural Change Work in Progress.* New York: Routledge.

Anderson, K. (2011). *Thinking About Sociology.* New York: Oxford University Press.

Anderson, R. J. (1994). Representations and Requirements : The Value of Ethnography in System Design. *Human Computer Interaction, 9*(3), 151–182.

Arnold, E., & Thompson, C. (2005). Consumer Culture Theory (CCT): Twenty Years of Research. *Journal of Consumer Research, 31,* 868–882.

Batteau, A. W., & Psenka, C. E. (2012). Horizons of Business Anthropology in a World of Flexible Accumulation. *Journal of Business Anthropology, 1*(1), 72–90.

Berger, P., & Luckman, T. (1966). *The Social Construction of Reality.* New York: Anchor Books.

Bhattacharjee, Y. (2013, April). The Mind of a Con Man. *The New York Times2.* Retrieved from www.nytimes.com/2013/04/28/magazine/diederik-stapels-audacious-academic-fraud.html?pagewanted=all&_r=0. (Accessed November 22, 2013.)

Boltanski, L., & Chiapello, È. (2005). *The New Spirit of Capitalism*. New York: Verso.

Bourdieu, P. (1984). *Distinction: A Social Critique of the Judgement of Taste*. Cambridge, MA: Harvard University Press.

boyd, d. (2007). *Why Youth (Heart) Social Network Sites: The Role of Networked Publics in Teenage Social Life*. Cambridge, MA: MIT Press.

Briggs, J. L. (1970). *Never in Anger: Portrait of an Eskimo Family*. Boston: Harvard University Press.

Bryman, A. (2004). *Social Research Methods* (2nd ed.). Oxford: Oxford University Press.

Bunzel, D. (2002). The Truth of the Organization: Simultaneity, Identity and Discipline in an Australian Hotel. In R. Whipp, B. Adam, & I. Sabelis (Eds.), *Making Time: Time and Management in Modern Organizations* (pp. 168–181). Oxford: Oxford University Press.

Burke, M., & Kraut, R. (2011). Social Capital on Facebook: Differentiating Uses and Users. In *CHI 2011* (pp. 571–580). Vancouver, BC: ACM.

Butler, J. (1999). Imitation and Gender Insubordination. In C. Lemert (Ed.), *Social Theory: The Multicultural and Classic Readings* (pp. 575–585). Boulder, CO: Westview Press.

Caron, A., & Caronia, L. (2007). *Moving Cultures: Mobile Communication in Everyday Life*. Montreal: McGill-Queens University Press.

Castells, M. (1996). *The Rise of the Network Society*. Malden, MA.: Blackwell.

Cefkin, M. (2009). Introduction. In M. Cefkin (Ed.), *Ethnography and the Corporate Encounter* (pp. 1–41). New York: Berghahn Books.

Chodorow, N. (1999). Gender Personality and the Reproduction of Mothering. In *Social Theory: The Multicultural and Classic Readings* (pp. 406–411). Boulder, CO: Westview Press.

Conrow, L. (2010). *Developing a Taxonomy for Office Email: A Case Study*. Master's thesis, Rochester Institute of Technology.

Creswell, J. W. (1994). *Research Design: Qualitative and Quantitative Approaches*. Thousand Oaks, CA: Sage.

Douglas, M. (1972). Deciphering a Meal. *Daedalus, 101*(1), 61–81.

Dreyfus, H. (1992). *What Computers Still Can't Do.* Cambridge, MA: MIT University Press.

——. (2009). *On The Internet* (2nd ed.). London: Routledge.

——, & Dreyfus, S. (2008). Beyond Expertise: Some Preliminary Thoughts on Mastery. In K. Neilsen (Ed.), *A Qualitative Stance: Essays in Honor of Steiner Kvale* (pp. 113–124). Arhus, Denmark: Arhus University Press.

Fine, G. A. (1993). Ten Lies of Ethnograhy: Moral Dilemmas of Field Research. *Journal of Contemporary Ethnography, 22*(3), 267–294. Retrieved from jce.sagepub.com/cgi/content/abstract/22/3/267. (Accessed November 22, 2013.)

Flynn, D. (2009). "But My Customers Are Different!" Identity, Difference and the Political Economy of Design. In M. Cefkin (Ed.), *Ethnography in the Corporate Encounter: Reflection on Research on and in Corporations* (pp. 41–57). New York: Berghahn Books.

Frank, R. (2007). *Richistan: A Journey through the American Wealth Boom and the Lives of the New Rich.* New York: Crown.

Gadd, C. S., & Penrod, L. E. (2000). Dichotomy Between Physicians' and Patients' Attitudes Regarding EMR Use During Outpatient Encounters. *Proceedings / AMIA ... Annual Symposium. AMIA Symposium,* 275–279. Retrieved from www.pubmedcentral.nih.gov/articlerender.fcgi?artid=22 43826&tool=pmcentrez&rendertype=abstract. (Accessed November 22, 2013.)

Geertz, C. (2000). *The Interpretation of Cultures.* New York: Basic Books.

Gibbs, P. T. (1998). Time, Temporality and Consumer Behaviour: A Review of the Literature and Implications for Certain Financial Services. *European Journal of Marketing, 32*(11/12), 993–1007.

Gilligan, C. (1993). *In a Different Voice: Psychological Theory and Women's Development.* Cambridge,MA: Harvard University Press.

Glaser, B. G., & Strauss, A. L. (1967). *Discovery of Grounded Theory: Strategies for Qualitative Research.* Chicago: Aldine.

Glenday, D. (2011). Power, Compliance, Resistance and Creativity: Power and the Differential Experience of Loose Time in Large Organisations Weber to Foucault. *New Technology, Work and Employment, 26*(1), 29–38.

Goffman, E. (1959). *The Presentation of Self in Everyday Life*. New York: Anchor Books.

Goncalves, E., & Fegundes, M. (2013). Reflections on Positionality: Pros, Cons, and Workarounds from an Intense Fieldwork. *Ethnographic Praxis in Industry Conference Proceedings*. London.

Granovetter, M. (1973). The Strength of Weak Ties. *American Journal of Sociology, 78*(6), 1360–1380.

Gray, P. (2011). The Decline of Play and the Rise of Psychopathology in Children and Adolescents. *American Journal of Play, 3*(4), 443–463.

Gwizdka, J. (2004). Email Task Management Styles : The Cleaners and the Keepers. In *CHI '04: Proceedings of the Conference on Human Factors in Computing Systems* (pp. 1235–1238). Vienna: ACM.

Hammershøy, L., & Madsen, T. U. (2012). Ethics in Business Anthropology. *Ethnographic Praxis in Industry Conference Proceedings*, 64–73.

Harper, R., & Shatwell, B. (2003). Paper-mail in the Home of the 21st Century. In R. Harper (Ed.), *Inside the Smart Home* (pp. 101–111). London: Springer.

Hine, C. (2000). *Virtual Ethnography*. London: Sage.

Hochschild, A. R. (1997). *The Time Bind: When Work Becomes Home and Home Becomes Work*. New York: Metropolitan Books.

Hutcheon, L. (2006). *A Theory of Adaptation*. New York: Routledge.

Jaruzelski, B., Le Merle, M., & Randolph, S. (2012). *The Culture of Innovation: What Makes San Francisco Bay Area Companies Different ?* San Francisco: Bay Area Council Economic Institute.

Jones, P. (2008). *We Tried to Warn You: Innovations in Leadership for Learning Organizations*. Ann Arbor, MI: Nimble Books.

Jordan, B., & Lambert, M. (2009). Working in Corporate Jungles: Reflections on Ethnographic Praxis in Industry. In M. Cefkin (Ed.), *Ethnography and the Corporate Encounter* (pp. 95–137). New York: Berghahn Books.

Jung, C. (1964). *Man and His Symbols*. New York: Dell.

Kimmel, M. (2008). *Guyland: The Perilous World Where Boys Become Men.* New York: Harper Collins.

Kluckhohn, F. R. (1953). Dominant and Variant Value Orientations. In M. F. & F. R. Kluhohn (Eds.), *Personality in Nature, Society and Culture.* (p. 346). New York: Knopf.

Kozinets, R. (2010). *Netnography: Doing Ethnographic Research Online.* Thousand Oaks, CA: Sage.

Kuniavsky, M. (2003). *Observing the User Experience: A Practioner's Guide to User Research.* San Francisco: Morgan Kaufman.

Ladner, S. (2008). *Agency Time: A Study of Time Reckoning in the Organization of Work in the New Economy.* York University.

———. (2012). Changing Time: Digital Calendars, Smartphones, and Temporal Transformation. Theorizing the Web Conference, University of Maryland; April 12, 2012.

Lakoff, G., & Johnson, M. (1999). *Philosophy in the Flesh: The Embodied Mind and Its Challenge to Western Thought.* New York: Basic Books.

Laxer, G. (1995). Social Solidarity, Democracy, and Global Capitalism. *Canadian Review of Sociology and Anthropology, 32,* 287–313.

Library of Congress. (2001, November 30). Margaret Mead: Human Nature and the Power of Culture. *Bali: Personality Formation.* Retrieved from www.loc.gov/exhibits/mead/field-bali.html. (Accessed November 22, 2013.)

Linton, R. (1936). *The Study of Man.* New York: Appleton-Century.

Liu, Z. (2005). Reading Behavior in the Digital Environment: Changes in Reading Behavior over the Past Ten Years. *Journal of Documentation, 61*(6), 700–712.

Lombardi, G. (2009). The De-skilling of Ethnographic Labor : Signs of an Emerging Predicament. Proceedings of EPIC, 2009, 41–49.

Ludwick, D. A., & Doucette, J. (2009). Primary Care Physicians' Experience with Electronic Medical Records: Barriers to Implementation in a Fee-for-Service Environment. *International Journal of Telemedicine and Applications, 2009,* 2:1–2:9.

Lundin, R., & Soderholm, A. (1995). A Theory of the Temporary Organization. *Scandinavian Journal of Management, 11*(4), 437–455.

Luxton, M. (1980). *More than a Labour of Love: Three Generations of Women's Work in the Home.* Toronto, ON: The Women's Press.

Malaby, T. (2009). *Making Virtual Worlds: Linden Lab And Second Life.* Ithaca, NY: Cornell University Press.

Margolis, A. (2013). Five Misperceptions about Personal Data: Why We Need a People-Centred Approach to Big Data. *Ethnographic Praxis in Industry Conference.* London.

Mariampolski, H., & Schlossberg, P. (2007). Ethnography Offers a Way to Know Our Customers Better. *Automatic Merchandiser, 49*(4), 40.

Martin, R. (2009). *The Design of Business: Why Design Thinking Is the Next Competitive Advantage.* Cambridge, MA: Harvard Business Press.

McClain, C. (1977). Adaptation in Health Behavior: Modern and Traditional Medicine in a West Mexican Community. *Social Science Medicine, 11*(5), 341–347. Retrieved from www.ncbi.nlm.nih.gov/pubmed/905844. (Accessed November 22, 2013.)

McCorkel, J., & Myers, K. (2003). What Difference Does Difference Make? Position and Privilege in the Field. *Qualitative Sociology, 26*(2), 199–231.

McCracken, G. (1988). *The Long Interview.* Newbury Park, CA: Sage.

McKenzie, B. (2011). *Commuting in the United States: 2009.* U.S. Census Bureau, Washington, DC.

Menzies, H., & Newson, J. (2007). No Time to Think: Academics' Life in the Globally Wired University. *Time and Society, 16*(1), 83–98.

Miles, M., & Huberman, A. M. (1994). *Qualitative Data Analysis: An Expanded Sourcebook* (2nd ed.). Thousand Oaks, CA: Sage.

Mills, C. W. (1959). *The Sociological Imagination.* New York: Oxford University Press.

Muzio, D., Hodgson, D., Faulconbridge, J., Beaverstock, J., & Hall, S. (2011). Towards Corporate Professionalization: The Case of Project Management, Management Consultancy and Executive Search. *Current Sociology, 59*(4), 443–464.

Mykhalovskiy, E., & Weir, L. (2004). The Problem of Evidence-based Medicine: Directions for Social Science. *Social Science & Medicine (1982)*, 59(5), 1059–1069.

Nardi, B., & Whittaker, S. (2002). Face-to-Face Communication in Distributed Work. In P. J. Hinds & S. Kiesler (Eds.), *Distributed Work* (pp. 89–113). Boston: MIT Press.

Nettleton, S. (2006). *The Sociology of Health and Illness.* London: Polity.

Nippert-Eng, C. E. (1996). *Home and Work: Negotiating Boundaries through Everyday Life.* Chicago: University of Chicago Press.

Oliveira, P. (2012). Ethnography and Co-Creation in a Portuguese Consultancy: Wine Branding Research as an Example. *Journal of Business Anthropology*, 1(2), 197–217.

Pateman, C. (1988). The Patriarchal Welfare State. In A. Gutmann (Ed.), *Democracy and the Welfare State* (pp. 231–261). Princeton, NJ: Princeton University Press.

Pine, J., & Gilmore, J. H. (1998). Welcome to the Experience Economy. *Harvard Business Review* (July-August), 97–105.

Pollack, J. (2007). The Changing Paradigms of Project Management. *International Journal of Project Management*, 25(3), 266–274.

Portigal, S. (2008). Persona Non Grata. *Interactions*, (Jan/Feb), 72.

Potter, G., & Lopez, J. (2001). General Introduction: After Postmodernism: The Millennium. In J. Lopez & G. Potter (Eds.), *After Postmodernism: An Introduction to Critical Realism.* London: Athlone Press.

Ramírez, R., & Ravetz, J. (2011). Feral Futures: Zen and Aesthetics. *Futures*, 43(4), 478–487. Randall, D., Harper, R., & Rouncefield, M. (2005). Fieldwork and Ethnography: A Perspective from CSCW. *Ethnographic Praxis in Industry Conference* (pp. 81–99).

Randle, K., & Culkin, N. (2009). Getting In and Getting On in Hollywood: Freelance Careers in an Uncertain Industry. In A. McKinlay & C. Smith (Eds.), *Creative Labour: Working in the Creative Industries* (pp. 93–116). London: Palgrave Macmillan.

Rattner, S. (2009). Why We Had to Get Rid of GM's CEO. *CNN*. Retrieved from money.cnn.com/2009/10/21/autos/auto_bailout_rattner_excerpt.for tune/?postversion=2009102103. (Accessed November 22, 2013.)

Reese, W. (2004). Ethnography for Business: Optimizing the Impact of Industrial Design. *Design Management Review, 15*(2), 53.

Rinehart, J. W., & Faber, S. (1987). *The Tyranny of Work : Alienation and the Labour Process* (2nd ed.). Toronto: Harcourt Brace Jovanovich Canada.

Rogers, E. (1995). *Diffusion of Innovations*. New York: Free Press.

Schultz, H. (2011). *Onward: How Starbucks Fought for Its Life without Losing Its Soul*. New York: Rodale.

Seeley, J., Sim, R. A., & Loosely, E. (1956). *Crestwood Heights*. Toronto: University of Toronto Press.

Shteyngart, G. (2010). *Super Sad Love Story*. New York: Random House.

Simmel, G. (1950). The Stranger. In K. H. Wolff (Ed.), *The Sociology of Georg Simmel* (pp. 402–408). New York: Free Press.

Small, M. L. (2009). *Unanticipated Gains: Origins of Network Inequality in Everyday Life*. New York: Oxford University Press.

Spradley, J. (1979). *The Ethnographic Interview*. New York: Holt, Rinehart and Winston.

Statistics Canada. (2011). Commuting to Work: Results of the 2010 General Social Survey. *Canadian Social Trends*, (August), 92.

Sunderland, P., & Denny, R. (2007). *Doing Anthropology in Consumer Research*. Walnut Creek, CA: Left Coast Press, Inc..

Taleb, N. (2007). *The Black Swan: The Impact of the Highly Improbable*. New York: Random House.

———. (2012). *Antifragile: Things That Gain from Disorder*. New York: Random House.

The Federal Reserve Bank. (2001). The Unbanked—Who Are They? *Capital Connections, 3*(2).

Thomas, D. (2008). *Deluxe: How Luxury Lost Its Lustre*. New York: Penguin Books.

Trotter, R. T., Needle, R., Goosby, E., Bates, C., & Singer, M. (2001). A Methodological Model for Rapid Assessment, Response, and Evaluation: The RARE Program in Public Health. *Field Methods, 13*(2), 137–159.

Tuckman, B. W., & Jensen, M. A. (1977). Stages of Small-Group Development Revisited. *Group and Organizational Studies, 2*(4), 419.

Tufte, E. (2003). *The Cognitive Style of PowerPoint*. Cheshire, CT: Graphic Press.

Tunstall, J. (1964). *The Advertising Man in London Advertising Agencies*. London: Chapman and Hall.

Turner, C. W., Lewis, J. R., & Nielsen, J. (2006). Determining Usability Test Sample Size. In W. Karwowski (Ed.), *International Encyclopedia of Ergonomics and Human Factors* (2nd ed., Vol. 3, pp. 3084–3088). Boca Raton, FL: CRC Press.

Van Maanen, J. (2003). *Tales from the Field: On Writing Ethnography* (2nd ed.). Chicago: University of Chicago Press.

———, Manning, P., & Miller, M. (1986). Editors' Introduction. In J. Van Maanen, P. Manning, & M. Miller (Eds.), *Sage University Paper Series on Qualitative Research Methods* (Vol. 1, pp. 5–7). Beverly Hills, CA: Sage.

Venkatesh, S. (2008). *Gang Leader for a Day: A Rogue Sociologist Takes to the Streets*. New York: Penguin Press.

Weir, L. (2008). The Concept of a Truth Regime. *Canadian Journal of Sociology, 33*(2), 367–389.

Willis, P. (1978). *Profane Culture*. London: Routledge.

———. (2000). *The Ethnographic Imagination*. Cambridge, UK: Polity.

Willis, P. E. (1981). *Learning to Labor : How Working Class Kids Get Working Class Jobs*. New York: Columbia University Press.

Wilson, R. (2010, July). Tenure, RIP: What the Vanishing Status Means for the Future of Higher Education. *The Chronicle of Higher Education*. Retrieved from chronicle.com/article/Tenure-RIP/66114/. (Accessed November 22, 2013.)

Ybema, S., Yanow, D., Wels, H., & Kamsteeg, F. (2009). Studying Everyday Organizational Life. In S. Ybema, D. Yanow, H. Wels, & F. Kamsteeg (Eds.), *Organizational Ethnography: Studying the Complexities of Everyday Life* (pp. 1–20). London: Sage.

Yoo, Y., Boland, R., & Lyytinen, K. (2006). From Organization Design to Organization Designing. *Organization Science, 17*(2), 215–229.

Young, M. W. (2004). *Malinowksi: Odyssey of an Anthropologist*. New Haven, CT: Yale University Press.

Zelizer, V. (2007). *The Purchase of Intimacy*. Princeton, NJ: Princeton University Press.

Index

About the Author

Sam Ladner is a sociologist who researches the intersection of work, technology, and organizations. She uses a range of social research methods, including interviewing, observation, ethnography, and survey research. She has consulted with Fortune 1000 companies on digital product design, organizational change, and the social aspects of technological innovation. She also trains and mentors designers, marketers, and account planners on research methodology. She has consulted with private-sector companies, including Citibank, Dell, GSK, VeriSign, and Genentech. She served as Postdoctoral Fellow at Ryerson University's School of Information Technology Management and has published in peer-reviewed journals. She currently works as a senior researcher at Microsoft on the Office Envisioning team, researching socio-cultural trends and helping design the next generation of productivity software. She holds a PhD in Sociology from York University and lives in Seattle with her husband and cat.